Kevin Pietersen on Cricket

The Toughest Opponents
The Greatest Battles
The Game We Love

Kevin Pietersen

sphere

SPHERE

First published in Great Britain in 2015 by Sphere

1 3 5 7 9 10 8 6 4 2

Copyright © Kevin Pietersen 2015

With thanks to Daniel Harris

A CIP catalogue record for this book
is available from the British Library.

Hardback ISBN 978-0-7515-6204-0
C Format ISBN 978-0-7515-6203-3

Typeset in Bembo by M Rules
Printed and bound in Great Britain by
Clays Ltd, St Ives plc

Papers used by Sphere are from well-managed forests
and other responsible sources.

MIX
Paper from
responsible sources
FSC® C104740

Sphere
An imprint of
Little, Brown Book Group
Carmelite House
50 Victoria Embankment
London EC4Y 0DZ

An Hachette UK Company
www.hachette.co.uk

www.littlebrown.co.uk

For Jess and Dylan, and the family and
friends who continue to support me through
this incredible journey

Contents

On Cricket   1

On Batting   11

On Building an Innings   31

On Limited Overs   57

On Fast Bowling   81

On Medium-Pace Bowling   105

On Spin Bowling   117

On Form and the Zone   159

On Pressure   181

On Captaincy and Leadership   211

On Conditions   235

On the Best   249

On the Future   267

Acknowledgements   279

On Cricket

I absolutely love cricket. Not as much as I love my family and my friends, but after that it's the best thing in the world and a constant in my life. That's why I'll do anything, forgive anything and put up with anything to play. I absolutely love cricket.

I've been obsessed with the game from a very young age. I was one of those kids who couldn't keep still, always fidgeting, and I'm still like that now – it annoys Jess, my wife, no end when I'm sitting at the dinner table. But when it came to cricket, I could actually sit and watch an entire Test match.

This probably had a bit of a wow factor for my mum and dad, so they encouraged me, and then when I started playing I found that I just loved everything about the game. I loved bowling, I loved fielding, I loved hitting the ball, and

I loved practising, so I started going to summer camp clinics that the KwaZulu-Natal players put on, where I got to learn a lot and ask a lot of questions.

In South Africa, you live an outdoorsy life, so spend most of the year playing sport. Winters are rugby and summers are cricket, which was always my focus.

To begin with, and for most of my teenage years, I wasn't especially good. I had some sort of a talent, I guess, and thought that I was okay, but mainly it was just what I enjoyed doing.

In the meantime, I grew a fascination for sportsmen. Because of the 1995 Rugby World Cup I really liked Francois Pineda, James Small, André Joubert, Os du Randt and Joost van der Westhuizen, but with cricket being my passion, Hansie Cronje and Allan Donald were proper, proper heroes to me.

With Hansie, I loved how aggressive he was when he batted, and I loved how he was with me when we met. I was seventeen or eighteen, and he called me over, saying, come and bowl to me – I've heard you can bowl a bit. He was just such a nice guy.

Allan Donald was obviously White Lightning, and wore that sunscreen across his face like warpaint. So as kids, when we played in the garden and stuff, we used to do the same. And like Hansie, he was just so aggressive, which made me think about the way I wanted to play and how the game should be played.

The more I played cricket the more I became fascinated by it, and the more I knew how hard it is, the more I wanted to get better. Every six deliveries, the ball comes down from a different person, from a different end, and the higher you go, the faster it gets – but you still only get one chance. As a bowler, if you don't bowl well you're out of the attack, but most likely, you'll get brought back later in the innings. If you're a batter, that's not the case, and the knowledge that once it's gone it's gone can be very hard to handle.

People like to say that cricket is a team game, but that's nonsense. Cricket is not a team game; cricket is a collection of individuals playing for a team. My numbers are my numbers, the fast bowler has his own numbers, and so does the spinner.

And cricket's not like other sports. In football, for example, a striker can not score but still have a good game, or a player can do nothing for eighty-five minutes, give the ball away, miss a penalty, whatever, then bang in a goal or make a crucial assist and end up Man of the Match. But if you're a batter and you nick off first ball or go on a bad streak, there's nowhere to hide. Obviously you can take a catch, but my role in the England team wasn't to take catches, it was to win games by making lots of runs. If I wasn't doing that, I was failing.

The mental application demanded by the game, how much of yourself you have to commit and engage, is definitely something that drew me to it. Cricket, although it's a sport, is not just a sport. Every day of a Test match poses a different challenge, and because there are five of them it's incredibly gruelling. If you're fielding, just hearing that bell before every session saps you mentally; it gets on your nerves.

And the more you fatigue, the more you've got to put in, the fitter you have to be to make something count at the end.

Setting up a Test match is one thing, finishing off a Test match is another. The intensity, variety and complexity of it all means that you can never relax. You're constantly thinking about the game, whether it's playing or training, when you go to bed, when you wake up in the morning. It keeps you going.

You've also got to be pretty intelligent to understand the situations you find yourself in, to navigate your way through them then react quickly and spontaneously to whatever's thrown your way. When I scored 149 against South Africa in 2012, I was whacking it about, and then at the end of the day Vernon Philander got the ball to swing. So I had to go right back into my bubble and knuckle down to start playing straight again, from fourth gear back to first, and then when it stopped swinging I thought, right, I can start attacking again. You just go through these little phases, especially in England, where overhead conditions change the pace of play, and that tests your ability to predict and adapt.

The best players are the ones who can do that, who can hold their nerve when it counts, and that's one thing I'm incredibly proud of. Throughout my career I've been able to absorb pressure and then put it back onto an opposition. In highly strung situations, I delivered a lot of the time.

For that to be possible, you have to respect the game and respect the beauty of the game. Strengths can be weaknesses – you might get out playing a favourite shot; the new ball seams and swings but also disappears quickly – and techniques are constantly evolving. Even if you're comfortable in yourself, your opponents will be working out new ways of challenging you, and you're also constantly dealing with your game; you're always mastering the art of batting.

Look at Kumar Sangakkara and Jacques Kallis. In the last eighteen months of their international careers, Sangakkara was Man of the Match in the World Twenty20 final, scored a Test triple century, two doubles, and proved he could succeed in English conditions; Kallis scored hundreds against England, Australia and India. Both of them kept developing, and like them I know I'm seeing and playing the ball as well as I've ever done.

The key to this is practice, because talent isn't enough. Practising, for me, is everything, and the only thing that can get you to where you want to be; you can't just coast on talent. I'm lucky that I have an obsessive nature – I'm a perfectionist, and determined to nail everything that I do. But what people often don't understand is that discipline and focus are skills, so need to be worked on too.

The only way to go from a net where you can get out twenty times into a game where you can get out zero times is to take it seriously every single time; there's no point trying different things and being reckless, thinking, tomorrow I can go out and play differently. It's just not going to happen. If you want to succeed in the middle, taking your practice into your performance is something that you're going to have to do. You've got to train your brain to know what you need to do and how you need to do it: that's the only way to survive in international cricket. I do everything possible to protect my wicket, and I always go hard.

That's how I got to where I am. I developed very late, and must have missed out on five or six years of absolute fun times because I wasn't particularly good between the ages of twelve and eighteen. But I worked incredibly hard at my game and my talent just grew and grew. The success I had once I came to Nottinghamshire in 2000 I'd wanted and earned over a long period of time.

I don't know what I'd be doing if I wasn't a cricketer, and the sacrifices I've made are why I'm so proud of being one. It was because I wanted so desperately to be a professional that I pushed on to the UK, where I knew that if I played well I'd have the opportunity to get the best out of myself.

Even now I'll do anything to play the game. I don't care what people say about me or do to me, because playing for England means more to me than any of that, and because playing for England is bigger than any individual. That's why I can't understand how people pick teams according to who they like. Ideally, I'd play in a team where everyone's a mate, but the reality is that it's almost never like that, and that's fine – people are different. Selection should be about one question: is he the best available for the position? That's it. I love and respect the game much too much and want to win much too much to demand anything from my teammates except ability and desire.

For similar reasons, I'm incredibly protective of the game; cricket's my baby. I guess I realised that for the first time when Hansie Cronje was caught match-fixing. The night before the story appeared in the papers, South Africa were warming up for a one-day series with a match against Natal, and I was playing. We all wondered why he ran off the field during the game, and then, the following morning, realised that he must have been told what was happening. It was unbelievably shocking and disappointing.

I'm not a person who has lived a perfect life. I don't think that anybody has the right to judge anybody else: if you make mistakes, you make mistakes. We all do, because nobody's perfect, and I was raised to recognise that. Hansie didn't murder anyone, and actually, he was always the same gentleman that I'd met those few years earlier. He obviously just loved money and got into the wrong scenario. So once he'd apologised and been punished, I was proud of how the country forgave him and happy that he could stay a hero.

But that doesn't mean I disagreed with his life ban. Match-fixing, spot-fixing – I'm fierce about anything like that. If you're caught you should never play again, because we have an amazing game. There are so many honest blokes out there, trying their hardest and committing to everything to make a living, and if you're cheating that then sorry, I'm afraid that's got to be it.

I know Mohammad Amir was only eighteen when he got into trouble, and that he was a special talent. I also know that he and Mohammad Asif, the best pace bowler I've ever faced, come from poor backgrounds and were offered a hell of a lot of money for a few seconds' work. But I don't care; they should not be coming back. I don't feel badly towards them and I wish them well in their lives, but the game is bigger than us, the game will be around a lot longer than us, and we don't have the right to steal from it. We play fairly, we play tough, we play positively, we play negatively, people play the way that they want to play. But there's no space in the game for corruption, and if you get caught you have to be given a life ban.

When the spot-fixing story broke in the *News of the World* we were playing Pakistan in a Test match at Lord's, and that day was the worst I've experienced in cricket. The guys didn't even want to bowl to them, we didn't celebrate the wickets that we took; everything about it was horrendous. We just felt so much anger towards them. We could not believe what they'd done.

But in general, the spirit between players is fantastic, and another amazing aspect of the game. Mainly, everyone competes and conducts themselves in the right way.

People talk about sledging quite a lot, and though it's not something I've always appreciated, these days I see it as part of the game, and a brilliant part of the game. When a bowler's in a batsman's face and he's having a go at him, it creates theatre, it creates entertainment. And I think that the authorities get involved too much these days – think back to Wahab Riaz and Shane Watson at Adelaide, during the 2015 World Cup. Incredible bowling and half an hour of the best cricket of the competition, which the umpires should have just left to carry on, because the whole of the planet was watching that battle, gripped and fascinated by it.

Mental pressure is part of the game. If a bowler can get into you that way, good for him. He might just need to stare at you, but he might also say 'I'm coming for you', 'You didn't play that too well, see if you can play the next one', or 'I'm going to knock your head off' – just those kinds of things, to start a bit of mental disintegration. It's completely unacceptable to abuse somebody for their personal life, but other than that, anything goes.

When it comes to walking, however, my thoughts are that if you know you're out, you walk.

Jimmy Anderson once asked me why I walk, and my response was simple: if I'm out, I'm out, and I've got no interest in pretending I'm not – I'll bat again another day. So if I'm sure, I leave as quickly as possible.

Yes, sometimes you can get away with it, but I've scored enough runs and I've had enough time at the crease. I enjoy my batting and I'm proud of it, so I want people to know that I play fair. It might not *technically* be cheating to stand your ground, but in my mind it is, and I've got no interest in that tag. I'd rather win the right way than the wrong way.

Maybe that's because, even though it's my job and I do refer to it as work, I still think of cricket as a hobby. A hobby that has given me the most amazing life and the most unbelievable opportunities to travel the world, see different cultures and make lots of friends. I do something that I love, something that I grew up as a kid loving, and I've done it for more than ten years. I've played 104 Test matches, and what do I do now? I travel the world playing T20 tournaments. If I can't love that and enjoy that, then I'm a fool.

On Batting

Like lots of complicated things, batting is really quite straightforward. Challenging, but straightforward. Greg Blewett, the first overseas professional that I played with at Notts, always used to say, you want to keep your batting simple: just watch the ball, and it's ridiculous how accurate that is, how something that seems so technical is hardly technical at all.

We're not clever enough to do much more than watch the ball – we can't be thinking about form and about the field at the same time. And anyway, you identify your scoring areas and your dangerous areas when you walk out to bat or pre-delivery. Subconsciously, you know where the fielders are, and they're not moving.

That happens because you've trained your brain for

exactly that purpose – but what you can't do is train it to know where the ball is. So once the bowler's at the top of his mark, just focus on that and nothing else.

That's what I did facing my first delivery in my first big international game, playing for England in South Africa, and with the volume of the Johannesburg crowd just insane. All I did was fixate on the ball. I can actually see André Nel running in right now, me watching and watching, before I played and missed. It was a bit of a nervous shot, but then I thought, there's nothing wrong here, and off I went in that series.

When I arrive at the wicket I mark my usual leg-stump guard and put my back foot on it square – though if I'm facing a spinner I open up my stance a little by bringing my right shoulder round towards the bowler. That's because I'm looking to be a bit more free-flowing, with a more natural swing through extra cover.

In the early part of my career I batted on the popping crease, but before the 2006/7 Ashes decided to move back ten inches and straddle the line. On the faster, bouncier Australian wickets I wanted a bit more time to position myself to play, and though we're talking about split-seconds, when you've only got split-seconds to start with anything extra makes a difference.

Once I'm set in my stance I get ready to face, starting with a knee-bend. I do that so that I'm loose, and also so I'm sure that I can move, because I know my legs aren't heavy. When the body is put under pressure muscles start to twitch, and that's why Ernie Els breaks his shoulders just before he plays a shot. What you then get is the Big Easy, one of the most natural, fluid swings in golf.

At the start of my career I was a really front-foot dominant player, because I wasn't playing against bowlers who could force me backwards with short-pitched deliveries. But once I started playing first-class cricket that needed to change, which it did when I got to Nottinghamshire and worked with the wonderful Clive Rice. He helped me develop a trigger movement, which gets me ready to go either forwards or backwards depending on the length of the ball that's sent down, and I've stuck with it ever since.

Basically, right as the bowler's loading up I go across my stumps with my back foot – the reason I start on leg is so I end up on middle, with my right eye on off. That way, I know anything outside it is outside the line, and anything in line or inside it is on the stumps.

At the same time, I'm concentrating hard on the ball and going at it with my head. That gets me into a kind of crouch, which I call the pouncing position, and from there I'm ready to strike, like an animal tracking its prey. It's something that a lot of batters do these days because you don't have time to do it all once the bowler's bowled – especially if he's really getting into you with short stuff.

Through release, I do everything I can to keep watching the ball and keep moving towards it with my head. The reasoning is simple: the closer your eyes are to something, they better they'll see it.

But your head's important, not just because it's where

your eyes are, but because it's the heaviest part of your body. Where it goes, everything else will naturally follow and flow, so if you get it into a good position your feet and bat will also find themselves in a good position. That's why, whenever I coach, whether it's kids or professionals, I just talk about eyes and heads. I'm not interested in foot movement, not interested at all.

What I'm not saying, though, is that everybody has to bat the same way. We're all different, and though most successful batters use a version of this method there's plenty of room for manoeuvre. You don't, for example, ever see me play the perfect cover drive with my elbow up like Ian Bell. But can I hit a cover drive? Yes I can. Why? Because, like him, my head is in the right position.

When it comes to actually playing the ball, my top and bottom hands do similar jobs. I grip the bat pretty softly because I'm a very wristy player. I know that's usually a description people associate with touch players and the cut shot, whereas I'm a power player who never plays the cut shot, but I use my wrists to help guide the ball to where I want it to go, by snapping them on contact.

The reason I don't cut is that I'm quick on the pull, and there aren't as many fielders on the leg side as the off side, where you've got a backward point, you've got slips, you've got gully. So if I get a ball that's short and wide, I'm either going through midwicket, where there might be one catcher, or over midwicket, where there's definitely no catcher.

Even so, more than a conscious decision, it's something that came naturally. Because I'm lucky to have long arms and a long reach, I don't need to move my feet that much, and I've always had the ability to get forward and drive on the up, at the top of the bounce. On the other hand, a lot of other players will have to wait for those balls, which is when they'll cut.

And, obviously, there's also an aptitude thing. For a long time, Steve Waugh didn't pull a ball or hook a ball – he really had lots of issues with that – but goodness could he cut! I can't, so I don't.

Ultimately, though, we can say whatever we like about physical and technical attributes, but it won't change the reality that the way you bat is a reflection of your personality. It's who you are. I guess that's one of the reasons I'm so protective of my approach.

I've got an incredibly upbeat attitude to life. I love it when the sun shines and people are happy; I love the buzz it creates. And that's what I'm thinking when I bat: be positive, have fun, entertain.

I'm also a pretty impatient person – I'm impulsive, and want things now. I just can't help it. I'll say to Jess, aw, I'd love to have that pair of shoes, and she'll tell me, if you still want them next week, get them. What do you mean, *if* I want them? What do you mean, *next week*?

It's the same in business. There are loads of things where I just think, why can't I have this when I've asked for it? Why can't I have it now? And obviously I understand that there's a process that you've got to go through, but it doesn't mean I can change how I am.

That part of my nature explains why I've done some of the most ridiculous things in my career, and why, even though I've learnt to hold back as I've got older, some of my dismissals have been pretty pathetic. But these same traits have also helped me do some pretty special things as well.

The funny thing is – and I can almost hear people sniggering as I write this – I'm actually an introvert. Whenever I've done the Myers–Briggs test, the results have always said I'm so introverted it's frightening.

I'm fascinated by how we categorise introverts and extroverts, because people so often assume that I must be an extrovert. But actually, extroverts are those who need others around in order to get their feelings out and express themselves, whereas I'm happy in my own skin and happy to be on my own. Throughout my career people have said, oh, he doesn't partake in team stuff – well no I don't, but that's because of my personality type. I'd rather be doing bits and pieces by myself than surrounded by lots of people and having to put on a show, or having to talk.

I guess it's possible that playing as I do is my outlet, but I think it's simpler than that. I just love batting, and the way I bat is the way I have to bat to be successful. I know myself very well.

Growing up, I wanted to be like Hansie, whacking spinners, playing his slog sweep. The problem was, I was far too skinny, so ended up an off-spinner instead. People ask me how I went from that to being an international batsman, and one of England's best ever in terms of numbers. There must have been a transition. I can only put it down to hard work, passion and – eventually – belief.

Basically, I knew I wasn't going to succeed as an off-spinner because, to get good, you need to bowl overs and overs and overs, and then to build pressure with maiden after maiden after maiden. I really didn't have the patience for that.

So I thought, right, how the hell am I going to improve my prospects as a cricketer, as a first-class cricketer, let alone an international cricketer? The only way was to add another string to my bow: batting. And the more I practised it, the easier it got.

When we were eighteen, Grant Rowley – my best buddy in South Africa – and I decided to spend the winter growing ourselves some muscles. We worked really hard in the gym in the morning and trained in the afternoon, five days a week for six months. So I got stronger, and then that summer, goodness, was I whacking balls: I started hitting sixes and feeling much more confident in the way I went about my business.

Nowadays, because I know I can clear the boundary, I train differently, and specifically for how I play. As soon as I feel heavy at the crease, I'm nowhere; I want to feel light and balanced, not like in 2005 when I was fat! So I look after myself – I eat well and don't drink much – and don't do any weights. I used to love running, but I can't do it any more because of the knee issues I've had, so I do a lot of work on the bike and in the pool, as well as on core stability, stuff like sit-ups and planks. But back in 1998 it was all about building power.

The following season I started to gain some momentum in my game, and in December 1999 played for Natal against the England touring side. I took four wickets in 55.5 overs, but more importantly, batting at number nine, I hit 61 not out with four fours and four sixes. I was starting to develop a style, and when I arrived at Trent Bridge, Clive Rice promoted me to number six and said, right, I want you to score runs for me.

Even in those early days, I operated according to the numbers 4, 3, 2, 1. When the ball's coming down, first of all, I'm looking to score four, then three, then two, then one. If it's in my area I'm smashing it; if it's not, I'm getting off strike, and only as a last resort am I defending.

That approach gets me into good positions, helps me feel comfortable at the wicket and puts pressure on the bowler. He knows that I'm coming at him, and I know that I'm looking to be positive in everything I do. In particular, I try to control the area within a metre of me: anything that lands there, I really get my head and hands into and my bodyweight through, because those are the deliveries that are hitting my stumps. The rest I can either leave or play with a lot less worry, because the only way I'm getting out is caught.

Again, I'm not saying that this is the best way to bat; it's just the best way for me to bat. If I'm being assertive I've got momentum, and if I've got momentum I can score quickly and heavily, which is why I'm in the team.

So when the bowler's running in he's not thinking to himself, great, I can just get on with my day job here and settle onto a length. Not against me. I'll be looking to knock him off it, which means, because of my reach, he's got to be pretty special to maintain his areas – there's only a very small square he can hit where I won't try to score.

As technique and personality are unique, individual things, I've never really tried to imitate how other players bat. Lots of people have compared me to Sir Viv Richards, and obviously I'm flattered – he's a superstar, an amazing legend and one of the greatest ever. But I've always wanted to be my own person, partly because people who don't do that wind up very unhappy, partly because I've got no choice. You've got to live your life the way you want to live your life, accept the differences in other people and just focus on doing your best.

The thing I do look at in other people is how they go about their business. If I'm at a sporting event, if I'm at Chelsea, say, many people will stand at the bar or wait until the last moment to take their seats, but I'll be outside watching the players. I have this fascination for watching people practise – I love it. When I was rehabbing my Achilles injury in 2009, I went to Chelsea's training ground in Cobham and found I was more interested in watching the guys prepare than I was in watching them play. I like to see how blokes operate when they're not on television, because that's what gives you the edge – that's what makes great sportsmen.

What I learnt was how focused they are. They turn up, train hard for a short period of time on specific things and then leave. That's something we got pretty good at as an England team when we were at the top.

Essentially, I'm fascinated by successful people and I love being around them. I love listening to people like Roger Federer, Cristiano Ronaldo and Rory McIlroy, to learn from their approach. They know how good they are, which is why their standards are so high, and they perform with such freedom.

Confidence can be mistaken for arrogance and that can rub people up the wrong way; I understand that.

But that's how I have to be. Batting is hard, and for me to produce the results that I want and need to produce, I have to have a certain demeanour. Call it ego if you like – call it whatever you like – the fact is, you don't walk down the wicket to Mitchell Johnson without it. It was the only way I could survive, let alone control Test matches for England, win Test matches for England and get the best out of myself.

Sure, I've got things wrong along the way, but how I am is the only way that I know how to be; it's the way I was brought up. I wasn't brought up thinking second is cool. I wasn't brought up thinking just taking part is cool. I was brought up to think, you turn up today and you win. That's what you do: you win, and whatever you have to do to win, you do.

You're there to win, but if you do badly and lose it's just part of life. You're not going to win everything. You're not. My mum and dad raised me to enjoy sport and to take pride in it, no matter which team I was playing for, because they wanted me to be happy knowing I'd done all I could, and that I'd demanded the highest standards of myself.

Those fundamentals I was raised with are still fundamental

to me now. Going hard to win helps you develop the mindset that lets you bat aggressively, and the guys who do that are the guys who people want to watch. I'm no different: I love the whacking of the ball.

So if Jos Buttler, AB de Villiers, Joe Root, Hashim Amla or Virat Kohli are in, I'm there, because they're free spirits who look to get after it, whatever the situation. I don't mean that they never alter their game – sometimes you're forced to defend more. It's just the way that they do it, not by going into their shells and leaving a lot of balls, but by being as upbeat as they are in everyday life.

Kohli and Amla are two international opposition guys I know very well, different and similar at the same time. Virat's just an absolute pleasure; I just love his confidence and his attitude, which, of course, is exactly how he bats. Obviously he hits the bad ball, but he can do the same to good ones because his wrists are excellent, letting him whack lengths through midwicket from outside off stump. And now, as captain of his country, he's showing the same dedication to attacking options: he backed Rohit Sharma, found a way to get five bowlers into the team, and led India to a series win in Sri Lanka.

I grew up with Hashim, so I've seen him through his whole career. When he started in international cricket he had a real weak spot for short bowling, but he stayed positive and worked incredibly hard, and now he's a world-beater. Maybe not the kind of guy you're scared will murder you, but he still will – he's the quiet destroyer, who does it really cleverly, respecting good deliveries, punishing bad ones, manipulating the field and tiring you out. There's a fine art to his batting.

Kohli and Amla both defend straight. They don't defend to gully, they don't defend to backward point. When they play a defensive shot they're in line, head in position and bat close to the body, whacking to mid-off or extra cover. If the bowler bowls and the ball comes right back at him, it sends him a message. It tells him you're hitting the right way, you're dictating, and he starts thinking, shit, I can't get past this guy.

On the other hand, when you start defending to behind the wicket and you hear the keeper and the slips constantly chirping 'Well bowled, half a bat, that's our half of the bat,' that gives bowlers the confidence and impetus to perform.

Very different from Virat and Hashim, but similarly talented, is Ian Bell. He's naturally a shy, reserved sort; a perfectionist – maybe that's why he always preferred batting at number five, a lovely position, to batting at number three, the hardest position, even though his technique is perfectly suited to the role.

When he's relaxed and on song you get the Ian Bell who starts on you, abuses you and takes the piss out of you the whole time. He's just a great, fun guy, and that's what you see in his batting: patches of absolute brilliance and intent. When he's playing really well he's like a little bull terrier nipping at your heels, and the more confident he is, the more his personality overcomes his insecurity. But then, all of a sudden, a couple of bad knocks and it's gone –

sometimes for a long time because of who he is. Batting is simple, but people are complicated.

So it's not as straightforward as saying what we've all said to him: mate, just score runs – you're that good! He's doing his best with what he's got, and the essence of what he's got can't change, however many Tests he plays. People like to say that he could have done better with his talent, but they're missing the point. His personality contributes to his good form as well his bad form, and one is clearly worth the other.

But in any case, the capacity for confidence is also a talent. Ian Bell could have done better if he were Brian Lara, but he isn't, he's Ian Bell, and Ian Bell has done as well as Ian Bell possibly could, which is magnificently well.

Confidence is important in all sports, but even more so in cricket, because it's so mentally and emotionally demanding. That's why, if you look at all the best players, the one thing you'll find they have in common is the ability to make things simple. It takes a lot of confidence to do that, to say that you're happy with how things are, but it means you can let your technique take care of itself and work on getting your mind right.

Getting your mind right is something that you learn. You've got to understand how it works, and how to switch certain parts of it on and off. Sometimes the emotional part looks out for you, saying, you don't want to get out here, because of this, because of that, and the trick is getting the logical part to reply: well, I've faced enough deliveries in these circumstances and I've conquered them before, so I should be able to conquer them today too.

Someone who is excellent at this is Alastair Cook. He at times is a worrier, but to his credit is able to say everything's fine even when it's not. As I know to my benefit – playing for England – and my cost – not playing for England – Cook is a phenomenally stubborn man. It's this, as much as anything, that makes him such a brilliant batsman, and also the type of batsman that he is: loads of character, not so much flamboyance. He has an amazing faith in himself, which is why he was so convinced he should be in England's one-day team, for example.

But, great player that he is, I have a frustration. Cook's a tall, strong guy – he loves his muscles. And yet he doesn't play a cover drive. Maybe he thinks it's a high-risk shot, but it'd be nice to see him have a go. He should be whacking the ball off the front foot, banging it down the ground like Matthew Hayden. But that's just not his personality, whereas with Haydos, it is.

Hayden and Cook also have the advantage – and it is an advantage – of being left-handed. Because the vast majority of bowlers are right-arm, over-the-wicket seamers, anything outside off stump they can leave, while anything that pitches on their hips they can tuck away. And they get plenty of those, because that's the line that gets sent down to right-handers.

I've spoken to Kumar Sangakkara about this a lot, and as a lefty he agrees that if you line up really well and play in straight lines towards the bowler or towards mid-on, you don't have to drive much early in your innings, because you can get your runs elsewhere. Basically, not many deliveries are hitting your wicket, so you defend the ones that are and the rest you can either leave or score from.

In the meantime, bowlers are getting a whole lot more impatient, which makes them go searching for things and sends even more balls towards the pads. Given how strong lefties are in that area, these often end up as boundaries, but a bad defensive shot does the job as well – midwicket, single, fine leg, single, not a problem.

A right-hander has to play at far more because far more balls – almost all of them – are starting on the stumps, or at least threatening them, so the lbw, the nick off and the bowled are all possibilities. On the other hand, if I've got a left-armer running in I know that, if I line myself up right, anything outside my eyeline I can just leave, unless it's really full, in which case I'll drive at it.

But even that isn't the same. Though they're a bit more fashionable now, there still aren't that many left-armers around, and you've generally not grown up playing against them – your brain isn't trained in the same way and the angle's always tough. You've got to change your set-up, your stance, and you've got to think about totally different things, whereas for left-handers, facing right-armers is totally normal.

And that delivery slanting across them towards off stump is a big part of the reason why lefties look so elegant when they bat; it naturally falls right into the slot for them to cover drive – for the purist, the most beautiful shot there is. The timing and precision of David Gower was something special, the way he caressed the ball, though the two most elegant players of my time are righties: Ian Bell and Damien Martyn. Just to watch them flow through the off side or flick through the leg side, and those late cuts as well – gorgeous! Just so much time, so much grace, the kind of thing you could hang in a gallery.

But within batting, within the art of batting, there's beauty beyond the shot. Beautiful batting is also not being over-dominant and not being over-confident, just manoeuvring balls to score freely while taking minimal risk. Kumar Sangakkara and Mahela Jayawardene are outstanding at this, master craftsmen able to impose their expertise on every form of the game.

Then there's Jacques Kallis, another beautiful batsman, but in a completely different way. Because he's so technically correct, he's got so much time to play, and he also has the mental capacity to bat for long periods of time and be strong, assertive and clever in the way that he builds his innings.

I know that my batting isn't like theirs. I'm fun to watch because I whack the ball, but I'm certainly not artistic in my method – it's more structured, more physical and more brutal.

But people are into different things, and again, when it comes to sport what really does it for me is how people conduct themselves in certain situations. Could they get through the toughest periods? In terms of my career, the

151 I got at Colombo in 2012 is the best example, because I never thought I could bat that long in that heat.

That's because, in the end, beauty isn't about what you see, but how what you see makes you feel. I know some people find that in stats, and as cricketers we're conditioned to obsess about them – they're what keep you in a job. So I can tell you how many Test runs I've got (8181), how many tons (twenty-three) and how many Man of the Match awards (twenty-six).

Obviously, I'm proud of them, but the reality is that they're only part of the story. Four fifties are better for your average than one 158, but it might just be that the 158 is more useful to your team.

And certainly more memorable. No one ever wants to talk to me about my numbers, they want to talk to me about how I played the game. They say things like 'Man, you whacked the Australians,' and 'Jeez, how did you play that innings in Mumbai?' and the knowledge that, in whatever small way, I made them happy is the most beautiful thing of all.

What I want from sport is the primal feeling that makes you buzz inside. When I think about my favourite players, I'm not thinking about how many, but about how. How they grabbed me and how they excited me, even when they failed. That's why I watch certain players and don't watch others, and why I don't care that, even though I love having him on my side, Alastair Cook's scored more Test hundreds than me, Viv Richards and Ben Stokes.

A good example of everything I've been talking about is the 152 I made at Lord's in 2008, in my first Test innings against

South Africa. We'd still not made our peace with one another, so I was under huge pressure, and the media were hyping things up as they do. I told myself that it was just another game, just another case of watching the ball and being able to deliver.

I was in such a good bubble, still in that early phase of my career when I was in the form that got me selected in the first place, that I more or less believed myself. I hadn't gone through tough periods and I'd managed to make a lot of decent contributions; the game felt very comfortable and very easy. So in a way, there was nothing special about the knock, nothing special about it at all; I got it like I got most of my other hundreds.

I came in at 117–2 with Strauss and Vaughan having gone in consecutive overs, and while I was still on 0 Cook also went. I then took a bit of time to get going, so Belly outscored me for a while, but I kept calm; there are certain periods of play when you can't be as forceful as you'd like, either because you're not quite there, or because bowlers are bowling well. But then I got going, found things easier and did what was normal for me at the time – played positively and tried to smash anything in my area.

Actually reaching my hundred, though, was not normal, even by the standards of getting a Test hundred. They're all incredible because they're so hard to get – people think you should do this and you should do that, but come on, how many people have got Test hundreds? How many people have played the game?

This one meant even more than usual, because of how

much I'd put into it, over years and years. Taking the step to leave my home, family and friends, build a life somewhere new and take all the flak of playing for a different country.

Obviously I celebrated well, with my customary 'Boom!', and ran and jumped down the track with a bit more craziness than usual. But the thing that will stay with me for ever is the applause, which just never seemed to stop. Even when I tried to take guard again, the crowd were still clapping and clapping and clapping.

And I thought, wow, I've finally been accepted into English sport! That was an amazing, unique feeling, it really was, because you always want to be accepted. The way I played to get that hundred, the crowd being the way it was and it being at the home of cricket was a truly beautiful – and simple – feeling. And for me, that's what batting is all about.

On Building an Innings

Building an innings sensibly is the key to getting runs. For me, it's mainly about looking for scoring options, but a lot of people talk about batting in the V, and that's wise advice. At any level of cricket, playing straight for as long as possible is what gets you in, and the fewer risks you take early on, the longer you're likely to stay at the crease. Then you can go from there.

Basically, you're looking to feel the bat on the ball, read the conditions and understand what the bowler and captain are trying to do to get you out. In international cricket you sort of know, because we play one another that often, and the field also gives it away – but it's always worth making sure and investigating whether there's anything new, so you can adjust your game as necessary.

In some ways, building an innings starts before the game. I don't make notes about other players, because I know what they do and I'm focused on myself, but I do keep notes on my phone about what I do when I'm playing well. Anti-corruption measures mean I can't take them with me into the dressing room so I look over things when I'm lying in bed the night before a game, or on the bus.

At the start of a series I read this, about how to start an innings:

Test batting bubble. Small trigger, staying leg side, thinking about me and not the bowler. Looking to go forward, but bearing in mind the short ball. Leave everything in the channel, play straight back at the stumps, play straight midwicket, only drive ball under nose until I've got the pace of the wicket. Low hands at the start means I've got a lot more control, get myself in after a break, don't be stupid and go after spinners straight away.

This if I'm facing spinners:

Defence is the key to any form of batting. Don't plant my feet, two strike zones, picking length, right-hander hitting the left-arm spinners through cover every ball. The off-side game, use bat and not pad to defend.

This if I'm playing in India:

Stay leg side, small trigger, same low backlift. Spinners, front press with a low backlift, quick feet, watch the ball off the bowler's mark, open up stance, bend my knees. Hitting sixes, low in the stance to get under the ball, stand perfectly still, weight going forward.

And this if I'm playing a one-day international:

Look to stand leg side and play off side. Face 30 balls, no reckless risks, value your wicket and remember that runs can catch up at the end, but above all watch the ball. Playing left-arm spin, stand still and tall, look to hit every ball through extra cover, wait to square leg, look to come forward every ball, easier to go back after being forward, open stance, track the ball.

When I'm waiting to bat I don't do visualisation or anything, I just watch the screen to find out what's going on. I look at the pace the bowler's bowling, what the wicket's doing and how the guys are playing, especially how they're scoring.

Obviously, what you see on screen is different from what you see in the middle, and because I've always batted so differently from the guys ahead of me – Marcus Trescothick, Alastair Cook and Andrew Strauss were all left-handers, for one thing – it was hard to work out exactly what I'd need to do.

But during intervals I could speak to the guys who'd already batted to find out how much the ball was swinging and seaming, whether it was spinning, and how easy or hard things were in the middle. Obviously if someone's just got out you leave them for half an hour, but after that you chat about what to expect. And although with that kind of information it doesn't matter whether they're right-handers or not, I always made sure I talked to Jonathan Trott.

When I first got into the Test team, we'd have the TV coverage on in the dressing room, which I liked. You've got so many knowledgeable, wise heads in the commentary box, talking so much good sense, that you could pick up little snippets to use which might help you win a match. I really enjoy listening to Nasser Hussain and the Channel Nine lot in Australia, like Mark Nicholas, Mark Taylor and Michael Slater. I also love Bill Lawry's voice, and always pay attention when Shane Warne commentates on my batting. It's just great how positive they all are about the game and about how you should play it – they make cricket sound so amazing and so attractive.

But when Andy Flower became coach in 2009 he wasn't so keen, and sometimes asked that the sound be turned down. I don't know if he thought there'd be too much information, or that it was a distraction, but I'd argue that if you want to be good at your job you need information, and whatever happens, you know you've got all these guys analysing you. I maintain it was a real shame not to have that.

Because people are different, they like to prepare in different ways – same as batting, it's dictated by your personality. Some are very serious – Cook and Trotty – and others need to have a laugh and a joke to relax – Matt Prior – but they're all trying to keep things as low-key as possible.

There are those who, when they're waiting to bat, sit calmly and just watch the game – Strauss, once he'd done all his stretches – and others who get really fidgety – Trott again. Me, I piss a lot, not because I'm drinking that much, but because I can't wait to get out there and I'm full of nervous energy. When I've had to wait hours, I've gone maybe ten times, but then once I'm out there not needed to go again for a whole session.

It's good, though, because nervous energy is a great energy; it means you care about what you're doing and are zeroed in on what you've got to do. And when I'm not in the toilet, I like to talk a lot: not about the game, just having a laugh with whoever's around.

It's an amazing sensation when the wicket before yours falls. Everything stops, and it's your time; there's nothing you can do now. You've got to put the worrying away and you've got to deliver. You've got to take your practice into the game.

As soon as I cross the white line I feel at peace, I feel free. I'll be saying to myself, wow, this is so cool, this is where I want to be, this is what I love. That's probably why some of my greatest innings have come when we've been in the most strife – if we're two down for nothing, or if two wickets have fallen quickly I've got less time to worry, to think and to watch, I just go out there and bat. Sometimes when we've been 300–2 and I've got out for nothing, it's because I've been sitting and thinking, oh my days . . . right, well this is how others are succeeding, I've got to do this, this and this, and got tired watching.

I don't feel like I've got a duty to entertain, but I do feel the weight of expectation on my wicket. I'm proud of that, but when I walk out to bat I don't think about it for a second. I'm only interested in the ball; that's the only thing on my mind and the only thing I go after. Do that, and the rest will follow.

Some people are very particular about their gear. I'm not. The bat I use is 2 lb 10 oz, which is medium, just a regular size. I make sure I've got a fair few in my bag so I know that if I break one I've got backup, but I'm not the kind of guy who has a practice bat and a match bat, and I'm not the kind of guy who looks after it like it's his child. A bat's a bat – I've got loads, and if one breaks I'll just use another one. I don't have a special bat, and I don't have any superstitions either. None.

Superstitions aren't for me. You get out of the game what you put into it. That I feel so strongly about this probably has something to do with growing up in a religious home: I think that everything happens for a reason, and what will be will be. That was drilled into me as a youngster, and I think it's helped me keep things as simple as I've kept them, and not to think if I've got a handkerchief and I scored a great hundred, I've got to keep that handkerchief in my pocket all my career. Bullshit. That handkerchief is not scoring me a hundred, what's scoring me a hundred is how well I practise, how good my head is.

If a little bit of fabric keeps someone positive and they think, I've got my little hanky with me, it's all going to be okay, and it helps them get their runs, then no problem – do that. It's each to their own, everybody's different. I just train hard and do my business; that's my thing.

That said, there is something about my batting that isn't logical, that I can't explain: I'm a feel player. What I mean by that is if I get out into the middle and the bat doesn't feel right in my hands, I know I've got a problem. The biggest battles I've had at the crease have been with myself, when I've taken my guard, got into position and just said, aw, shit, I'm not picking it up well.

It's so weird. Some days I'll be in my stance and think, good luck to the bowler, other days I'll think, no hope. The bat just has to feel good in my gloves when I pick it up, and when it doesn't, there's not much I can do about it.

When that happens, I tell myself, okay, today might not be my day, but can I get through it without sacrificing my wicket or getting out? But it wasn't something that I could ever really do. I'd tap my bat, pull out of my stance, get back in and remind myself to watch the ball, but I'd be so frenetic, with so many things going round in my mind. I'd be thinking, how is this going to be? I'm not holding it right, my hands are all wrong, my legs feel heavy – and then *boom*! It's just over so quickly, and you're on your way back to the pavilion.

Against South Africa at the Oval in 2012, I walked out in the second innings, picked up my bat, and thought I'd be lucky to last three balls. I nicked my twelfth to Kallis, who dropped it, and it took another five for Morné Morkel to knock my stumps out of the ground. Then at Headingley two weeks later, I got to the crease, took guard, and thought, I will murder South Africa today. It's amazing, absolutely amazing, and I've got no way of explaining it. It's just something that happens.

After that, and even though it's a relief to get to the crease, I'm still pretty jumpy before I get my first run. Partly, it's a weird thing about cricket and cricketers: in the same way that a century isn't just one more than ninety-nine runs, it's much better to see a 1 next to your name than a 0. But it's also the way we think as humans: it's a huge release to know that you're off the mark, especially for someone as impatient as me.

My thing has always been to hit at mid-on and sprint. I know people think it's dicey, but to me it's an easy run and doing it has never cost me my wicket. And it's actually a tactic I use throughout my innings, especially early on when I'm looking to punch down the ground, always presenting the full face of the bat until I'm in.

As I explained, the key to batting is head position and playing the ball as close to your eyes as possible. But what tells you how to do that – whether to go back or come forward – is what length it is. If I can, I try to get forward whatever, but in general, if it's full you go forward and if it's short you go back.

The ability to pick length is the key to batting – it's what the best players in the world do better than the rest. It's why tail-enders often struggle with short balls and yorkers, and even those of them who can play shots are still tail-enders.

What you need is good eyesight, so your brain knows what's going on as early as possible and can calculate what to tell your hands and feet to do. Even if you can't explain it physiologically, that's what's going on.

But though the ability to do that is a talent, you get good at it by practising regularly and hard, and that's what makes you special. Us batters spend hour after hour working at our games and repeating the crucial things to ourselves: pick length, move your feet, wait for the ball.

That's what I'm concentrating on when I'm facing. But you can't focus all the time, so usually as soon as I've played the ball that's me done. The opposition generally let me be when it comes to sledging, because they know that if they engage me in a verbal battle it will only get me going. Instead, I'll look at the crowd before locking myself into focus-mode again. Then I'll have a quick squiz of the field, going from third man all the way round to fine leg, and saying in my head, right, you're there, you're there, you're there, you're there, you're there, you're there, so my gaps are *bom-bom-bom* and that's where I'm going to hit. Then I remind myself about the situation of the game, how I can make things difficult for the guy running in, and get back into my stance.

I don't target particular bowlers, because I think on any given day I can club anyone – except for Mohammad Asif and Muttiah Muralitharan, the only opponents I never thought that I could control. All the others, I know I can go at: it's just a case of working out when's the right phase of the game.

Usually, I'm looking to hit four along the ground, as that's the safest route to runs – unless I'm facing a spinner, when the aerial route becomes an option too. Against seamers, though, I never really try to hit over the top until I'm in.

Always looking for the attacking option doesn't necessarily mean that I'm going to hammer a fast bowler through the covers, or even punch my defensive shots. Look at how Hayden and Ricky Ponting used to leave the ball: they went all the way forward, so their footwork needed to be just as good, got their hands right up and out of the way and gave a loud call, making it a real positive stroke.

And that's something that I developed in my game. I want to pressurise the bowler and show him that even though he's bowled his best ball I've still tried to score off it and am in complete control.

Of course, I'm not just showing this to the bowler; I'm also showing it to myself. The more confidently you do everything the more you convince yourself that everything's good, which helps you make everything good.

Early in my international career I didn't have that kind of calmness; I used to force things. That's why, when we went to Pakistan and India in the winter of 2005/6, I got a lot of starts but only one hundred. I was young, so just didn't evaluate or bat situations as well as I learnt to, and I made a lot of mistakes. Because I was playing high-risk cricket I nicked off a bit, was caught sweeping quite a bit, and even managed to get out pulling just before lunch. My average for the winter was 34.75.

But as you get older, you get better. The more you sit on a couch and relax, the more settled you are in your personal life, the more patient you can be on the field. You understand people better, you see different perspectives, you make better decisions.

Now, I adapt my game to circumstance – but only up to a point. The cricketers I hold in highest esteem are the ones still able to play their way in high-pressure scenarios, and if you start changing that, changing the person you are, you're going to come unstuck.

Even so, it's a very hard thing to do, which is why Adam Gilchrist was such a freak. Attack, counter-attack, whack the ball, that's it. Obviously you can't go in and try to hit your first ball for six when a bowler or a team are on fire; you knuckle in there for a good ten minutes longer than you would if you were 300–2. But after that, you can take it on.

And that's what I've tried to do too. People are picked to play certain ways and I don't think I was ever in the team to block – there were others who did that. I've always been there to take the attack to the opposition, even when we were on the back foot, because by playing shots I would force them to think about doing things differently, and to do things they didn't want to do.

Obviously people knew this about me, so sometimes they'd try boring me out. And Michael Clarke certainly did that in the 2013/14 Ashes, getting Peter Siddle to bowl a very tight line and, especially when Nathan Lyon was on, setting defensive fields with deep square leg, two extra covers, two midwickets, deep cover point, cow corner and long-on. Basically, he was saying, right, if you want to hit a boundary, you're going to have to go over their heads, and so the big battle for me was to see if I could defeat them on the ground. Siddle got me out twice in the second Test at Adelaide, then for 19 in the first innings of the third Test at Perth, where we ended up needing to bat out five sessions for a draw.

I came in at 62–2, and conditions were good. I got myself in, I was seeing it pretty well, and the bouncy track meant that I could hit through the line and on the up. So I did. I got to 45 off 87 deliveries, with six fours and a six that I smashed off Lyon. Then I tried to do it again because the ball was there for it again. I didn't quite get enough of it, it held up in the wind and Ryan Harris took a brilliant catch to get rid of me.

Obviously I'd have preferred not to have been out, and my score was in the range where I tell myself off afterwards because I'd got in but not cashed in. So I asked myself why it happened, and whether I'd played the wrong shot, but kept coming back to my role in the team.

Even my rear-guard innings – 158 at the Oval in 2005, 92 at Brisbane in 2006, 101 at the Oval in 2007, and 81 at Centurion in 2009 – were counter-attacks, coming at strike rates of 84.49, 59.35, 63.52 and 56.65. My career strike rate is 61.72, and people seemed to appreciate that.

In all my time playing for England, only once did I get told off for playing my game – that day in Perth. I came back to the dressing room and was on the balcony when suddenly Graham Gooch started shouting at me: what the fuck do you think you're doing? You've just hit a six and you get holed out on the boundary? I just listened and said, okay, fine. No worries, yep, okay. But inside, I was upset and pretty angry.

In the same Test, Shane Watson had been hitting Graeme Swann into the stand, *bang-bang-bang*, and George Bailey did the same to Jimmy Anderson. That's the new cricketing manual. But Gooch maintained you need to be technically perfect, get your foot to the pitch and hit along the ground; that you shouldn't take risks or take on boundary fielders.

But few would argue the game's changed; the game's changed in the time I've been playing it; the game's changed in the last three years. I grew up with the same textbook that Gooch did, but the Woodworm bat I used when I started is tiny compared to what I use now, which lets me hit the ball over the boundary even if I don't middle it. So it doesn't matter as much if long-on and long-off are out there – you still try whacking sixes, because you can be sure that somebody in the opposition will.

In front of me on that day in Perth was an average off-spinner I'd already hit for six, and a short boundary. Why wouldn't I go again when the ball was there for me? People talk about the great hundreds I've scored, and that's how I got them: batting in that same way. Without Perth, there would be no Oval, Colombo, Headingley or Mumbai. So I was thinking, they've been hitting Graeme Swann, a much better bowler; they've been hitting the leader of our attack.

That's what's going to happen, so we need people to go after them in return.

But all Gooch cared about was runs – he loved to say 'It's not how, but how many'. Which, even if were true (which it isn't), showed that he didn't get that my *how* and my *how many* are connected. Sometimes, even when you're fighting to save a game, it can be the speed at which you score that reverses momentum and saves you.

Anyway, who's to say that it's worse to get out playing a shot than padding up to a straight one like Cook would do in Sydney? Who's to say that me batting my way didn't give Ben Stokes the confidence to then go out there and deal with the Aussies like he did? And that's not me claiming the credit – as I said at the time, Stokes is a star – but we'd been under the pump for the whole series, and I was the one who started taking the attack to them.

I get that it was a stressful period, because it was for all of us – I was in serious pain and probably shouldn't have played. Even now, I'm gutted that my knee wasn't right, and had it been I'm sure I would have got a lot more runs for the team.

Gooch knew all of that, and he also knows me. I'll say it now, it hurt. I'm a sensitive guy, with emotions; I take my game seriously and always strive for perfection. I hoped he would just have said, you've played your way, that's how you've played your cricket – don't worry.

I'm just not into regrets. I regret not playing golf throughout my career, but that's about it. Shit happens – so what, just try not to do it again. You need to keep perspective. In cricket, there are going to be bad days and good days, and there are going to be more bad days than good days, whoever you are: I've played 104 Tests, but only scored twenty-three centuries. That's how it is. There are seven billion people in the world, lots of them suffering, and the world is just a speck in the galaxy; nothing I do is that important. Just enjoy yourself, enjoy your life.

If I want to really nail myself, I can think back to the occasions when I let myself down by not capitalising on starts, but I don't like doing that and it's not how I get the best from myself. I prefer to remember that in 2000 I was just an off-spinner, then I converted into a batsman and ended up getting more than thirteen thousand international runs. Relax, buddy.

So the next day I spoke to Gooch. I said to him, you've got your views on the way that you want people to play. This is the way that I play. Please don't speak to me like that again. Everybody was so on edge; it had been such a stupid time to go at me. Even Cook said, mate, don't worry about it.

Then we went to Melbourne, where the track was much slower and wickets were falling around me. In my younger days I might have gone for it anyway, to make a point and because that was what I did, but I chose not to. Like at Perth, I played my natural game relative to what the scenario presented, so made 71 off 161 balls and 49 off 90, getting out in both innings trying to whack it when I was running out of partners.

Meanwhile, the suggestion in the media was that I was some sort of luxury for the team, fine when things are going well but unreliable when they're not. But in fact, if you look at my career, the majority of my best innings have come when we've been in trouble.

There's something about coming to the wicket when you're in trouble that's different from when you're not. Those are days when I've picked up my bat and gone, phew, I can get runs today, when I've found the conditions easy, been confident and just been batting very, very well.

But there's more to it than that. Because I've always kept things so simple, the harder the situation the more I'm aware of it. If I'm walking out to bat at 3–2 or whatever it is, I'm going, right, you've got to zone in here, and that's all there is to think about. That doesn't mean I'm not zoned in at 300–2; my highest Test score, my 227 against Australia at Adelaide, I came in at 176–2. But I do take extra special care over getting myself in when we're up against it, which I think is human nature. In the same way that it's more of a buzz playing than training, and it's more of a buzz playing Australia than Bangladesh, it's also more of a buzz batting when you're in strife. And I'm able to turn that adrenalin and intensity into focus.

Otherwise, though, my method is the same every time. From the start, I'm looking to get fielders to where I want them, especially if spinners are bowling. So I'll play them through the off side as much as possible, to get an off-side field, and then I can hit them through the leg side, where

I'm very strong. But really, there's so much space out there, no matter where people are standing.

Obviously there's a battle with the opposition captain, but for me it's more about getting into the bowler's head so that he bowls me more bad balls, and I do that by stopping him doing what he wants. I have great battles with Dale Steyn because I never let him just run in and send down his beautiful outswingers. Instead, I use my reach to hit him as hard as I can, low through midwicket, fielder there or not, and anything short I murder, or try to murder. That's how I combat how good he is: by whacking him.

The more you manipulate the ball around the field the better. Bowlers hate singles being scored off their bowling and they hate people rotating strike, because that means it's the batsmen dictating play. And you don't just do that on your own, but with your partner.

Take Paul Collingwood, for example. Not technically the greatest player, but I loved his mental toughness and the way he went about his business. At Adelaide in 2006 he scored 206 against Shane Warne, Glenn McGrath, Brett Lee and Stuart Clark, and we batted together for 84.1 overs, the equivalent of almost a whole day's play, scoring at 3.68.

Because I'm a front-foot dominant player who hits on top of the bounce, against me bowlers need to bring their length back, or else they're giving me full tosses and half volleys. But to Colly – and Ian Bell – you need to be a lot fuller, making them come forwards because they want to go back.

Anything even marginally short is getting cut or pulled, balls I'd be hitting through the covers or midwicket.

That meant that when the two of us were in together bowlers had to vary their lengths by about a metre depending on who was facing, and that's not easy to do. It's one reason that, in forty-five partnerships, we averaged 60.04.

I'd be standing at the non-striker's end, enjoying Colly benefiting off balls that bowlers should have been bowling to me, and then I'd benefit off balls they should have been bowling to him, each of us scoring off different deliveries and in different ways. To me, that was a thing of absolute beauty.

Most of the time, the talk in between overs is just about what's going on: what the bowler's doing, where individual scoring areas are, what to watch out for, that kind of thing. You might start chatting to the bowler, playing on his weaknesses as he's trying to do to you, but otherwise everything happens so quickly you don't pay much attention to stuff that isn't your batting and the time just passes.

Jonathan Trott was really good to bat with; I enjoyed batting with Trotty. He'd occupy the crease, take the shine off the ball and put bowlers into their second and third spells. Trotty's also a great guy and we get on really well. One thing I found hilarious about Trotty was how he would always talk the aggressive option, but never play the aggressive option. He'd say, right, I'm going to come down the pitch and whack that spinner over his head. I mean, that's the way. And I'd reply, come on, Trotty, I know you're not going to do it, and he didn't. But it was important that he thought he would. His mind was telling him to take the aggressive option, which got him into good positions to defend and find the gaps, and that was how he scored so many runs.

What was also good about Trott was the fuss he made of himself before every ball, fidgeting, scratching his mark on the crease and generally making the bowler wait. He's a real perfectionist and incredibly meticulous, so takes great care of his kit and was exactly the same in the middle. He's just one of those guys who is really, really, really zoned in, and it was funny to see the opposition carry on while he paid no attention whatsoever; he was so in his zone and in his bubble that he'd just do what he needed to do and that was that. I loved playing with Trotty.

Alastair Cook is similar, just a great player – I'd say that of the players I've played with for England, the greatest were him, Jimmy Anderson, Freddie Flintoff and Graeme Swann. Cook's mental strength is phenomenal, the way he can stand there only playing the shots that he wants to, for hours and hours. And that made him great to bat with. He just inflicts so much pain on the bowler, because he bats and bats and bats and bats, grinds and grinds and grinds and grinds, which made it easier for us playmakers to attack.

Then, at the other end of the spectrum, is Michael Vaughan, a free spirit who encouraged my free spirit both in what he said and what he did. He hammered the short ball, played a lovely cover drive and didn't think too seriously about it. That didn't mean he didn't care – he did, he just didn't play as though he was worried about things.

Andrew Strauss came somewhere in the middle. He got into the team a year before me, and that was probably his best period – he batted superbly when England won in South Africa in 2004/5.

But a lot of players have wonderful starts to their careers because bowlers just don't know where to bowl to them; it's only after a while that you find out if they can really play. And Straussy could play. He got two great hundreds in the 2005 Ashes, especially the one at the Oval when the pressure was really on, and the hundred he got at the Gabba in 2010 was also excellent – he played some very, very good innings. He cut and pulled well, drove down the ground well and generally looked for the positive options, even more so when he was captain. I guess that's because he's naturally a worrier, and if he hadn't made that 177 at Napier in 2008, he'd probably have lost his international career for good. So he really benefited from the sense of security the captaincy gave him; it meant he was sure of his place so could come out of his shell and play differently.

Apart from Colly, though, my favourite batting partner was Ian Bell. Partly because of how beautifully our styles meshed, but also because of what we achieved together. Our 350 partnership against India at the Oval in 2011 is England's seventh-highest of all time, but the 115 we put on in the third Test of the 2013 Ashes was a lot more important.

The first game at Trent Bridge ebbed and flowed, with Belly's century making the difference – we had an important partnership there too, of 110. But after losing at the last, Australia then collapsed at Lord's, and we absolutely battered them by 347 runs.

It was different at Old Trafford, though. A proper flat Test wicket meant that only the best bowlers got something out of it and our quicks couldn't, so Australia made 527–7 declared. If Graeme Swann hadn't taken five-for, we'd have been even more screwed.

By the time we batted, the pitch had deteriorated a little, but they also had the extra pace of Ryan Harris and Mitchell Starc, with Peter Siddle and Shane Watson keeping things tight. I came in with three wickets down, as Trotty had sent Tim Bresnan in as nightwatchman, only to be out there himself before the close of play.

I've always taken a nightwatchman myself, so I totally get why you'd have one – who wants to get out in the last six overs of the day? The fielding side are really fired up, and it just takes the stress away, it's a huge release of pressure. You can feel the burden on your back and you're thinking, jeez, I'd really rather not, so as soon as the six-over mark comes down and somebody else takes over, you take your pads off and think *ahhhh* ... But what I've never understood is why, if you're going to use a nightwatchman and he gets out, you don't send in another. But we didn't. Trott went in and survived, was out early the next morning, and then it was my turn.

When things were going well, we'd be laughing and

joking in the dressing room, with music playing. But because we were in a bit of trouble it wasn't as loud during that innings, and there was a bit of a tense atmosphere.

That had me super-focused on doing a decent job. I said to myself, Joe Root faced fifty-seven balls but only scored eight runs; he's a right-hander, what were their tactics to him and why did he find it difficult to score? Are they bowling it straight, what are my scoring options, and why are we 64–3 on a pitch they did so well on?

Walking out to the middle, I'm really, really buzzing, because I've not been in great form, and I know that we're at a stage in the game where somebody has to stand up and just get us through that spell. When you lose a couple of quick wickets momentum is with the opposition so you've got to try to look like you're in control even if you're not.

I plan to play with confidence and purpose, but it's easier said than done. Ryan Harris is bowling beautifully, running in and covering the ball so I can't see which way it's reverse-swinging. Right away I play and miss at one outside off stump, then just manage to get bat on an inswinging yorker that I'm lucky to nick to fine leg. I'm worried.

But then I get myself in. I get off the mark with four to fine leg off Siddle, and because the pitch isn't quick enough to bowl proper bouncers, when Starc tries I pull him for four twice in two balls, and think, here we go, we're on here.

So I get to thirty with a mixture of boundaries and nudges before going after Lyon, hitting him over the top for four and then for consecutive sixes. That makes him set the field back, which means I can rotate the strike pretty comfortably, and by that time Bell's in, and he does the same. He's in incredible nick, everything's just so easy for him.

My feet are moving well against the spinner, I feel comfortable at the crease, and only Harris is giving me any trouble – he's still in the groove and it's him I'm really, really watching. It's no surprise that it takes him to get Belly out, clean-bowled for 60 when I'm on 83.

Two fours and four singles get me to 96, and then Starc gives me some width, so I smack him over cover to get my hundred – not a shot I play much, just my impatience again. In the West Indies in 2009 I went from 83 to 97 by taking Sulieman Benn for four, four, six, then top-edged behind trying to get to my ton. And because the IPL auction was happening a couple of days later, people were calling me Dumbslog Millionaire.

I look back now and laugh: 97 was better than what everyone else got, and I was no Michael Slater, who was famous for getting out in the 90s. It did happen to me five times before March 2010, though, so I guess it was around then that I learnt to control myself.

It's funny, because most of the time I'm not worried about my score. I'm just worried about watching the next ball. And that should be even more the case if I've got to 90, because it means I'm in good form and there's nothing to worry about. In 2010 I made 80 against Pakistan, and I still don't know how I did it, I was playing that badly, but I've never got to 90 without feeling relaxed. Somehow, though, the milestone brings pressure, and much as you tell yourself that there's no need to stress, another ten is no problem, you also think, well, I could sort this out in one or two shots, and then you try . . .

Getting to your hundred is just an amazing feeling, a relief and a thrill at the same time, and looking around Old Trafford, seeing how happy people are, I feel like I've saved our bacon and helped us take a massive step towards retaining the Ashes. I feel invincible because as a batter it's my job to get hundreds, and when I do, the release of pressure is insane. They say the easiest time to bat is after that, and it's certainly true for me. I'm literally thinking, I've dealt with this bowling attack and now it's my time to just enjoy being here.

I always make sure to remind myself to enjoy those moments, to take them in, take the crowd in, and then just to relax – but I'm so excited that I need to regroup. It's an easy regroup, though, because I'm watching the ball, I'm focused on the ball. And often, when someone's made a century the bowlers aren't trying as hard as they were, because they're trying to attack the other guy, they're trying to get you off strike – especially in my case, because they know I'm going to get after it.

But even though I'm still rushing – and I rush for a long, long time – I'm saying to myself, you've got a hundred, now make it a big hundred. Make it a big hundred. Sometimes, tail-enders get hundreds, but tail-enders don't get 150s or 200s, and though I only got three Test doubles, of my twenty-three tons only four were less than 110 and ten were 150 and above – joint highest of anyone who's played for England, with Wally Hammond and Sir Len Hutton. This time, though, I don't manage it: Starc gets me lbw for 113 not long before the close.

I've never been one to shout, scream and carry on when I've had a bad day, and I've never been one to shout, scream and carry on when I've had a good day. The best players in the world are calm and level-headed throughout their careers, so that's what I try to do. You just enjoy that personal glow inside, which means you can rest easy.

But the thing about that Test was that it was a bit of an anticlimax. We were saved by the rain on the last day, so retained the urn in a game we were outplayed in, in the dressing room, with hardly anyone in the crowd.

Then at Durham the next week we were in trouble again and on edge for a long time. Going in for tea on the fourth day the chat was that if we didn't turn ourselves on, Australia were going to beat us and be in with a chance of a 2–2 draw. But somehow, Stuart Broad produced one of those spells like he can do, when he's absolutely unplayable, winning us the match and the series.

But even so, it wasn't that great a feeling. At the Oval, Michael Clarke's declaration set up an exciting finish, which was ruined by the rain.

It had been a good but not great summer for us – we got the better of certain situations, which is why things went our way, but I knew that Australia were coming back at us and would be much better at home. The main problem, though, was the fact that we had to do the whole thing again just a few months later. Our win was already irrelevant.

I remember talking in the dressing room, saying that players would go in and out of form, but when a bloke's running up to bowl to us at Sydney in January 2014 we'd know what ball he was going to bowl because we'd have played against each other that much. And that isn't how it should be. Ashes series are supposed to be really special, built up like an Olympic Games and with everyone peaking especially, but those ten Test matches were a complete shambles.

On Limited Overs

At last it seems everyone is agreed that Twenty20 is brilliant. It's brought lots of new people to cricket, kids love it and it's improved every aspect of the game.

In the beginning, and even though it was international competition, I was very much of the opinion that T20 was just a fun dance: turn up, have a slog, go home. But once people started throwing serious money around, it became a serious business; guys realised that if they got good at T20 they could do really well out of cricket. So they started to concentrate more and show more care for the format, not just in how they played and practised but also in how they thought and talked about it.

It might not have been the plan, but thanks to the riches of the Indian Premier League in particular, as well as the Big

Bash and Caribbean Premier League, cricketers from around the world play together, learn from each other and get better. Batsmen are looking for positive shots, driving, pulling and whacking spinners more, so bowlers have been forced to think harder and develop different balls – but also have better opportunities to take wickets. As a consequence, the fifty-over game is almost unrecognisable, and the five-day game is also a lot faster, with Test matches rarely petering out into boring draws. What we're getting is great for the game, and certainly the kind of cricket that I want to play and people want to watch.

Look at a player like David Warner: super-talented with great hand–eye coordination and no fear. He started in T20 cricket, whacking it around, making his debut for Australia before he'd played a first-class game. And if you can be seriously successful in limited overs you've got the ability to be successful in Tests, because you still need to have that basic technique.

Warner does. He's always had a pretty tight defence, playing the ball under his eyes and in line with his body, but that isn't enough. No chance. There are no bouncers in T20, no big spin, and far less pressure on your wicket.

So Warner defended more balls, and in 2014 ended up smashing South Africa – who probably had the best attack in world cricket at the time – on their home turf, averaging 90.33 for the series. It was a far bigger achievement than his second-innings runs in the Ashes immediately before it, because we were broken and behind, but that still had to be done too.

In a way, the prototype Warner was Virender Sehwag, who I know from our time with Delhi Daredevils. He's a great man and a wonderful batsman, who just thinks *boundary, boundary, boundary, boundary*, and doesn't think that spinners should be allowed to bowl; if anyone sends the ball down to him that slowly, he's not having it. And I love that about him. So in team meetings it was just 'Smash him,' 'Leave him', 'Smash him', done. I loved that positive attitude, I loved batting with him, and I loved spending time with him.

Sehwag actually made his Test debut batting at number six, and made a century, but the space was only available because India were trying Rahul Dravid as an opener. When that didn't work, first they moved him down to seven and then, before a tour of England in the summer of 2002, Sourav Ganguly asked him to have a go at the top of the order. It's so typical of Sehwag that, even though he'd never done it before, it made no difference whatsoever – he went and played his game there, then took it to T20 later on.

The best players just adapt, they play situations well, and if you've got the aggression and skill to hit over the top in the first over of a Test match, then why not? Opening the batting in five-day cricket, there'll be three slips, a gully and probably no cover, so why can't you whack through there? If you nick one, you're more likely to get caught, but if you've got the ability to hit the ball, hit the ball. If you can score hundreds in T20, then you can score hundreds in Tests, and if you can handle the pressure it's actually easier, because fields are more attacking. That's the new mindset, and it's brilliant.

But it's wrong to blame that mindset for how players got out in the 2015 Ashes, especially when not that many of them even play T20. Joe Root does and he went well, Ian Bell got his runs by attacking, Ben Stokes and Jonny Bairstow had their moments – but Jos Buttler failed because he went the other way, reining himself in. For Australia, Warner made scores, just didn't cash in, and Steve Smith batted time at Lord's; his struggles against the moving ball aren't because he plays in the IPL and Big Bash.

Australia didn't capitulate because they played an attacking brand of cricket. That's rubbish. Australia capitulated because there were other things going on; the dressing room clearly wasn't right. So when they got out into the middle they weren't happy, they didn't believe in what they were doing and it didn't look like the care factor was really there either.

If you look at the top ten batsmen in Test cricket – at the time of writing, Joe Root, AB de Villiers, Steve Smith, Hashim Amla, Kumar Sangakkara, Angelo Mathews, Younis Khan, Kane Williamson, Chris Rogers and Virat Kohli (Warner is ranked eleventh) – they are all, with the exception of Rogers, excellent T20 players and can play positive, exciting cricket in every format. That's because to be the best at T20 you need to understand the art of batting. Look at Chris Gayle, the best around, or Shikhar Dhawan and Murali Vijay. They play themselves in, then catch up later by playing proper cricket shots.

A few of those guys are openers, and that's a position I really enjoy in limited overs. You get two new balls that run away quickly, and also the full benefit of the fielding restrictions. On most grounds in the world, as soon as you beat the ring you're getting four, whereas if you come in later there's a sweeper on the boundary.

But wherever I am in the order, my method is the same: get to ten balls playing positively and in the right areas, and go from there. Ten balls is enough to get myself in and judge the pace of a wicket, and I'll always take them, even if I'm playing on a track that I know against people I know. Different bowlers do different things in different conditions on different days, so I'll always have a look at things first.

After that, I play every delivery the same way: to get as many runs as I can from it. But I never set targets. If I'm seeing it, I'm seeing it, and the runs look after themselves, but even if I'm not, I've never played my cricket thinking, we need 150 on this wicket to be safe. I've always just played as positively as possible. It's pointless to decide what a good total is, because it changes all the time with the size of the guys' bats and the way the guys bat. Par scores aren't par scores any more; you just need to get the biggest you can.

Most people seem to get this – none of the good coaches and captains ever decide how many runs they need. But when 'data' became the buzzword, it all changed. They'd be going over data and all that kind of thing. There were so many team meetings with a guy we called Numbers, Nathan Leamon, and he'd be telling us, this is what we should get, this is what an average total is, this is what a winning total is, but it's a waste of time. Just bat. Just keep it simple and whack it; that's it.

For similar reasons, I've absolutely no interest in the swing coaches people are into at the moment. Personally speaking, I can hit over the boundary and I can hit 360, so don't need to mess with my method and be more like a baseball player. But more generally, I find it pretty scary when people start overcomplicating things, because I worry about where it's all going to stop. Certain players can just play in a certain way, and you can either hit sixes or you can't. You don't have to hit the ball a hundred yards either; hit it seventy yards and it's still six.

That's all the more so given how big players' bats are these days. You hear quite a lot of talk about that, but I'm not fussed about it at all. If you can pick it up and you can smash it, do it. I don't stress too much about what other people play with, and I don't think anyone else does, apart from the commentators. They never used a bat that big, so they're probably thinking, if I'd had that in my day, what could I have done with my career? These guys have got it easy with these huge railway sleepers. Well, the fact is, that's what they've got and that's what they're going to use – times move on. You'll still nick off, you'll still get bowled, you'll still be trapped leg before, and who's to say that a safe shot you could play years ago won't get you caught now, because the bat's that good?

In limited-overs cricket the balance between bat and ball doesn't matter. There's always going to be a positive result, so it always exists. No one wants a Test match in which both teams score six or seven hundred, but if totals are high in ODIs or T20s, the bowlers who can take wickets or restrict scoring are crucial.

That's why T20 has seen the development of new skills and approaches. The slower-ball bouncer is something that's come into the game in the last few years, and bowlers are varying their angle of attack a lot more, by coming around the wicket and using the width of the crease – anything to give the batsman something different to think about.

And that's great for both parties. I'm sure the bowlers I played with would have benefited from the IPL, because it's impossible not to, and that's why I tried so hard to get them involved.

The one thing that T20 has almost taken out of the game, though, and which needs to come back, is the genuine yorker. I talk about it in all the franchises I go and play in, because if someone bowls you a good one you've got to play a damn good shot to get it away. And whatever that shot is, unlike with a wide full toss, a cutter and all the other variations, you'd better not miss. As a fielding side, you should always look for the wicket-taking option, and that's what a yorker is.

The problem is that bowlers are scared of getting it wrong. If it ends up a length ball batters can hit it; if it ends up a full toss it's going straight for six. But Lasith Malinga is the best death bowler in the world because he bowls brilliant yorkers. And, talented though he is, he wasn't born a perfect yorker-bowling freak. If you watch him train, all he does is run in and hit a cone on a yorker length, over and over again, and Fidel Edwards is learning the same thing now. You can train your brain to be specific about what it does, so you can train it to zone in on the spot you need. It can be done. You've just got to practise it, and it's useful in all forms of the game.

I feel slightly differently about other deliveries. I know that bowlers have improved their slower balls and cutters, and they're useful as change-ups, but in general, even in limited-overs cricket, you get better results by keeping things simple. Bowl top of off stump, make players play in areas that they don't want to and attack their weaknesses – or try to turn their strength into a weakness, with a line and a field that tempts them to take you on.

Another advantage of franchise tournaments is that you become familiar with different conditions, so that when you play international cricket abroad you know what you're doing. Look at Ben Stokes, for example: great against fast bowling, but weaker against spin and on slower tracks. Why? Because he's grown up playing county cricket, where they prepare result pitches, and conditions, especially in the early part of the season, demand seamers.

But even if you sorted out the county game, if you're serious about learning the art of playing spin bowling, you've got to go to the subcontinent. Send Stokes to the IPL and see how quickly his Test batting improves, especially against off breaks and the ball slanting across him. I'd scored Test hundreds against Muralitharan and Warne before I had my issues with slow left-arm, and what fixed them? My friendship with Rahul Dravid and watching how great players train – basically, the IPL.

And it's not just conditions in the middle that need getting used to; touring India is like touring nowhere else. The IPL gives you a home city, a home ground and a bunch of mates, so that when you come back with your country you'll feel much more comfortable, and you'll probably play better because of it.

The same applies to the Big Bash – I absolutely loved getting to practise and play at the MCG, to play at the SCG, the WACA and the Gabba. For an England player, there's no more intimidating place than Australia: the people there hammer you, and I've had it more than most. Crucified on the boundary, crucified in hotels, crucified by taxi drivers, crucified in bars, nightclubs and restaurants. But now I call Melbourne one of my second homes, because of how much I love the place and how well I get on with the people there. Australia is an amazing country and Australians are amazing people, but I needed to play in their domestic tournament to be able to appreciate that.

What helped a lot was that I was given the opportunity to commentate: the public saw me talking cricket with their legends, another thing they've got right in that competition. The people who call the game should have played the game, and it's only my generation and younger who've played T20. The Big Bash has Ricky Ponting, Adam Gilchrist and Andrew Flintoff, blokes who know what's going on; even

Mark Waugh, the selector for Australia, came in to have a laugh, and he's a proper great.

Overall, it's just brilliant to be a part of it, and once you start sharing a dressing room with the Australian players, the intimidation kings of world cricket, you think, seriously? Why was I worried about him? They're just great lads who love doing what they're doing.

But no one's benefiting from the IPL as much as the Indians, their young players especially. It's an amazing academy for them, and it's giving them so much confidence – every half-decent batsman is whacking or trying to whack Steyn, Johnson, Morkel and whoever. So if they ever get picked for internationals they know exactly what to expect, and they're definitely not going to be scared.

Meanwhile, in their own dressing room, there will be legends of the game showing them how it's done – how to train, how to prepare, how to compete and how to win. If they're smart, in those six weeks that they're with those guys they'll target them to find out exactly what they need to do to move their game forward.

I played with Virat Kohli when he was a youngster, and the thing that struck me most about him, apart from his talent, was how keen he was to ask questions, and his ability to learn. He'd want to know if I had any tips on batting, what to do in particular circumstances, how to play under pressure. I wouldn't say that I taught him anything, because he's a superstar, but I did talk to him about positive intent – reassurance more than anything, because that's who he is.

Playing for St Lucia in the 2015 CPL, I worked with Keddy Lesporis: he'd found himself trying to hit every ball on the on side, and because of that had difficulty driving. We looked at his method and discovered that his grip was very rounded, so when he lifted his bat in his stance it was angled towards leg. I got him to move his top hand a little bit further around the handle towards his body, which opened up the face, and now he's hitting through the covers.

A year earlier, I'd had similar with Andre Fletcher; Matt Maynard, our head coach, came to me and said that Fletcher could really play, but was struggling in the nets. I watched him for a while and saw that he was very lazy at the crease, so worked with him on his head movement and just being busier in his batting. That's partly technical – not just standing there going, oh right, the ball's been delivered now, I'd better move, but properly tracking it – and partly mental – looking like you've got energy when you're facing, and instead of waiting for something to happen, making something happen.

Because he's a little superstar, he then went and made 78, did well in domestic competition and improved again the following season. Batting together for the Zouks against the Barbados Tridents, we smashed 138 off seventy-five balls, and every time we came together in the middle of the pitch it gave me a huge amount of pleasure just to give him a fist bump or say, great shot buddy, outstanding, after he'd hit the ball out of the ground.

I see encouraging young players as part of my job, and I know it gave Andre an unreal amount of happiness and pleasure to bat with me – he says I'm his hero, his role model. I'd have been the same if I'd ever got to play with Hansie, and I did get to play with Shaun Pollock for Natal. Against Northern Transvaal at Kingsmead, we just started slogging together, we absolutely whacked them, and it was the best feeling of my life, the most incredible buzz. Not only was I hitting the ball, but I was doing it with a guy who was the captain of South Africa. It was amazingly special.

But, though I've given a couple of examples where I've given and received technical help, most of the stuff you pick up at franchise tournaments is to do with your mental game. The biggest thing for me has been seeing the positive attitude that the big players have, and seeing how simple they keep everything. It just reminds you that the way you're doing things is right.

Sangakkara is incredibly meticulous in the way that he practises, and he uses the same simple drill that I do with eight- and nine-year-olds: an underarm chuck. He just makes sure that he waits for the ball, gets his feet into position but doesn't plant them, then bangs it into a certain area, over and over, until he's happy that he's nailed it.

I do that too. I know I'm playing well when I wait to hit the ball under my eyes and I'm very particular; I don't move on until I'm satisfied. Sometimes, people can't see what that could possibly be doing for me, but it's teaching me discipline. This is the easiest thing in the world, but am I disciplined enough to hit exactly where I want to hit? Am I good enough? You see Sangakkara, you see Kallis, you see all the great players – they do the simple drills and they do them well.

What you also get from franchise cricket is a load of mates – which is obviously good for us, but also good for the game. You get fascinating scenarios where blokes are competing against their buddies, which makes for friendlier but more intense rivalries. Because, much as you like the guys off the field, when you meet in international cricket you want to nail them, and can't have them nailing you.

Before the 2013 Ashes, people told me I had to go right at the Australians, David Warner especially. But I was thinking, I can't abuse this bloke – I play with him in India. I've spent so much time with him, I know that, actually, he's a cool dude.

Of course, if he steps out of line and you've got to defend one of your guys you do, but there's no way I'm just going to go out there and start on him – what would I want to do that for? He's my buddy, at the end of the day. That isn't more important than being a teammate, but if I know that having a go him isn't going make any difference there's no point.

But however much I love franchise cricket, the highlight of my T20 career so far was helping England win the 2010 World Twenty20 and being named Man of the Series.

Leading up to that tournament, I hadn't been in great form. I'd come off a one-day series in Bangladesh where I wasn't batting especially well and was really struggling against the spinners. But then, on the outfield in Dhaka, I went and did a simple little drill with Mark Garaway, just using a really low backlift, because when you've got a low backlift a lot less can go wrong, and I started punching the ball, punching the ball, punching the ball . . . and something clicked. That one session took me to a place that allowed me to average 83.33 in the Tests there, then I went to the IPL, spoke to Dravid and averaged 59.00, the highest in the competition.

So when I went to join up with England, I was in a great place. Dylan was about to be born, and all the guys were buzzing: we were in the Caribbean and everyone was having fun.

Though not for one second did we think we could win the whole thing – no chance. We wanted to, of course, same as every tournament, but we were England and that wasn't what England did.

Then we started to play some brilliant, carefree cricket. Graeme Swann was amazing, Ryan Sidebottom was magnificent, Craig Kieswetter did well, I had the tournament of my life, and when you've got three or four players in that kind of form you stand a good chance.

Sidebottom, when he opened the bowling, was especially tricky. In the nets he always used to hit my inner thigh, pinning me in between my pads, and it became a bit of a joke between us. On a couple of occasions I got him, but when he had the new ball on a green wicket it was very, very testing.

I didn't do great in the first couple of games, but then I made 73 not out against Pakistan without worrying about batting or runs at all, because I knew they were coming. That told me I was right there, and I was in the same space when we played South Africa in Barbados. I remember it clearly: I batted beautifully that day, taking Morkel for 19 off ten balls and Steyn for 23 off eight, whacking him onto the roof of the pavilion. I ended up making 53 off thirty-three and we won pretty easily.

There was one shot in particular that I played off Steyn, a slap through extra cover, that I hit especially well. It's a bit like an inside-out tennis shot, because the ball seems like it's going straight but ends up going wider. Basically, it's a case of getting your head into a good position, so that even if your feet aren't moving you can use your wrists to dictate which way you hit. Keep them firm, play through the line as you would with a classic drive and it goes towards mid-off; break them on impact and it goes through extra cover. It's a technique used by a lot of batters from the subcontinent, Sehwag in particular.

In the final we played Australia and, amazingly, beat them pretty comfortably. Kieswetter scored 63, I got 47, and we had the mother of all parties to celebrate. Along with winning the 2005 Ashes, it was my proudest moment in cricket.

As for fifty-over cricket, I fear for its longevity.

I understand why people want it – TV pays, and it gives you eight hours, not the three and a half that you get from T20 – but as time goes on the sport gets fitter and faster, the players need more of a break between matches and it could be at the cost of one-day cricket. We all agree there's got to be enough time for players to recover, to recuperate and to spend time at home, and there's got to be enough time for franchise tournaments because you need the best players playing in all of them, just as the best players need to play in all of them – they're the most profitable element of a short career.

The bottom line is, T20 cricket is going to be here for a long time. And because it is already the game's most popular format as far as audiences go, it puts pressure on Test cricket. So we need to find the best way of protecting it.

What you don't want is to have the best players choosing between Test cricket and T20, or international and franchise competition – you want them available for everything. But for that to happen the workload needs to be lighter. The fifty-over game is something that puts quite a lot of strain on the players – it's a hell of a long time to field. I know that the 2015 World Cup and England–New Zealand series were excellent, but that quality is rare, and people are fickle.

In England, we're very lucky that the support is always there: people see going to the cricket as a day out, a day away from work – it's a social occasion. But in other countries people have less time and money, which is why T20 is so popular. It brings them the full package of excitement, condensed into a three-and-a-half-hour time slot, and you still get to see the best players in the world performing.

The format benefits the players too, because you can easily play back-to-back matches if you want to. You can't do that with ODIs, because it's just too taxing on the body.

As a result, you end up away from home a lot and with a six-week World Cup, which is just stupid.

That said, the fifty-over game has improved in recent years – thanks to T20. You've still got the striking phase, the rebuilding phase and then another striking phase, but the passages are less defined, and sometimes the whole innings can be a striking phase.

But whatever you do, you've still only got one chance. The more risks you take the more chance you have of getting out, and maybe that's why, good though the World Cup was, there weren't very many close games and even fewer high-scoring close games.

It doesn't give me any pleasure writing this stuff; I'm just trying to be practical, and I'm really not trying to club the fifty-over game. After all, it gave me my start in international cricket.

I was first picked for England when we went on a one-day tour of Zimbabwe at the end of 2004. Andrew Flintoff and Marcus Trescothick were being rested, and Steve Harmison ruled himself out for political reasons, so Belly, Simon Jones, Matt Prior and I were included for the first time.

I did quite well: 27 not out and 77 not out in the first two games, didn't bat in the third, and was out for a duck in the fourth. Then, at the start of 2005, I played in the one-dayers that followed our Test series with South Africa. It was always going to be tough, and Duncan Fletcher had wanted to keep me away from it. But Freddie got injured, I replaced him, and batted beautifully when we warmed up against

South Africa A in Kimberley; my 97 off eighty-four balls earned me a spot in the team for the first ODI.

This obviously caused a lot of fuss, but I've got to say I really enjoyed the rivalry and the hostility: I've always played better in a confrontational environment. And the natural confidence I have in myself means that I've always wanted to test myself, I've always wanted people to think, jeez, when it was tough, he came to the party.

Well, now I could and they could too. South Africa was the most intimidating environment that I'd ever played in, and gave me a real buzz. Before the serious games had even started, I remember getting excited and thinking, shit, if I do okay here I can set out my stall to have an amazing international career.

And then I said to myself, I have to be strong here. I cannot be a wimp. Because I'd made some remarks about South Africa which I now know were silly, stupid remarks, me talking about the quota system and how rubbish it was for the country when I really didn't understand the dynamics of its society.

The older I get, the more I understand that it's good for South Africa to give people not just fair opportunities but, in certain circumstances, more than fair opportunities. At the time, though, having said all those things, I knew I needed to back them up and prove my point: that I was ready to play on the biggest stage. And I also wanted to play well for all my friends and family who'd supported me coming to England.

Kimberley was a huge confidence boost, and when I was picked for the first game all I did was remind myself of Greg Blewett's watch-the-ball advice. Then, before the first game in Johannesburg, on the outfield at Wanderers Stadium, we got into a huddle and Michael Vaughan said, guys, we know and we understand that KP's in for a hell of a ride over the next two or three weeks from the crowd. If anybody goes at him, if you hear anybody go at him, you fucking support him like he's your best mate, because we are a team, we are a unit, and we are going to fight like fuck.

That made me feel incredible. Michael Vaughan, the great Michael Vaughan and the captain of the team, was treating me like his mate. Treating me like his mate and asking everyone else to back me through a situation that they knew was going to be difficult. And I felt that support in the team; I felt it around the lads. Alex Wharf and Gareth Batty, to name a couple, were magnificent on that tour; I got on so well with those guys. Darren Gough, Ashley Giles, Vaughany himself, Marcus Trescothick, they really were a great crew; I felt really proud to be their teammate. And Vaughan and Duncan Fletcher looked after me and took the pressure off – the sign of true leadership.

But the crowd were really fierce. Vaughany said that he'd try his hardest to keep me off the boundary, but it was actually quite amazing, the first time a boundary rider went out at extra cover I swept there, and jeez, did I get some abuse. 'You traitor, you traitor! How could you say those

75

things about South Africa? Fuck off back to England, we don't want you in our country!' All that kind of stuff.

Even though Mum and Dad loved the fact that I was playing for England, they were visibly upset when I got the abuse that I got. Which is understandable: I'm a parent now, and I don't ever want my son to be attacked like that. Mum, despite being incredibly proud that I was playing for the country of her birth, has said to me that was very hard for her. As all mothers are, she's understandably very protective and hurts when I hurt. Perhaps more so.

But leaving South Africa was definitely best for me. I've learnt a lot of things, I've grown up, I've matured, I've made mistakes. But I've got an amazing life, I've got an amazing family, and my three brothers all live in England now. England is home; it always will be. And I wouldn't want it any other way.

I'll never forget the first ball that André Nel bowled me. I was nervous, I was beaten by a ball that I could have nicked, and my whole story could have taken a different path – but it didn't. I missed it, thought, the pace is okay, I'm obviously in good enough form, and then managed to play well, get some runs – 22 not out – and we won on Duckworth–Lewis.

I actually got on well with the South African players; there were no real issues with them. No one really went at me apart from Graeme Smith, which is fine – it's what happens on a cricket field, and we're mates now. He'd be saying stuff like 'You don't want to fuck this up, you've got a chance,' 'Everybody's here to come at you, you don't want to nick off for nothing now,' and 'You think this is loud? They'll abuse you even more when you're walking off the field.' Nothing major, just little bits and pieces to try to encourage some mental disintegration.

It was much harder to ignore the crowd. So I listened to them, took it all in and then brushed it off, but they were quite difficult to forget when I was by myself at night. Closing my eyes, with my head on the pillow, I'd hear them again. I'd be going through the day, trying to break it down and figure out exactly how it went and how I played, but all I could think of were the things people had said to me on the boundary.

That kind of thing does affect you as a sportsman, definitely. So I tried to use it to my advantage, thinking, you know what? I've made a decision here. I've got to try to make this decision count. Which meant producing on the field.

Luckily, I'd practised well and was batting well – I found it pretty easy on that tour, even coming in in tricky situations. I got a 108 not out, a 75, a 100 not out and a 116, but in the end it was worth nothing: we lost 4–1, and it was especially demoralising to tie in Bloemfontein, where I scored my maiden international ton.

I took a lot of confidence back to England, though, because I'd found no bowler too good for me. Shaun Pollock was an amazing cricketer, but was coming to the end of his career, and, by chance, it happened that Makhaya Ntini's action was perfect for the way that I batted. He'd run in tilting to the left and angle the ball into the stumps from wide of the crease, with no outswing but a really nice skid, so I found real comfort and ease hitting him through my favourite midwicket scoring area without any risk. I loved facing Makhaya.

The following summer, England played two Tests against Bangladesh. I wasn't selected, but they hung around until Australia arrived, and we played an ODI tri-series. These days, you tend to play fifty-over games after the Tests, but this was much better for us because we wanted to lay down a marker for the Ashes and get a look at the bowlers we'd be facing.

I'm sure that for spectators it's hard to get excited about an ODI series no one will remember once it's finished – and for the players, it can be difficult. Mentally, you just can't get yourself up for it. But schedule it before, and it really stokes the fire.

In 2005, Fletcher and Vaughan were very forceful in setting out their plan to be aggressive – they even had us throwing in every ball hard, to show that we were tuned in and ready for the fray. We weren't going to be bullied, and we were going to attack. If the Aussies gave us something we would give it to them back; we weren't going to be just another English team that got trampled. We wanted the public to see us as battlers, and we believed that, if we did everything we planned to, the talent and maturity we had in the squad meant there would be a very close contest.

In the T20 at Southampton, we absolutely smashed them – I made 34 off nineteen balls – and then in the first ODI they made 252, a reasonable score at the time. In response, we got off to a bad start – I came in at number six, behind Collingwood and Flintoff, when we were 119–4 and needing 134 to win from 22.4 overs. It was quite a stiff ask, but it was a case of just playing well, not worrying about being dismissed or keeping up with the rate. I was young and new in the team, but I was also in decent nick, so just needed to watch and hit the ball.

Knocking it around for a little bit to get the pace of the wicket, I found that I could pick Brad Hogg's chinamen. And then, because the pitch at Bristol was that good, I was able to accelerate by hitting balls into areas I found comfortable; everything was good.

On 34, I actually thought I'd been run out, when I took a quick single to Ricky Ponting at mid-on and he hit the stumps with an incredible throw. But, somehow, the ball rolled across them and only dislodged the bails once I was home.

After that, I had a little row with Shane Watson – nothing special, he was just giving me some abuse and he bowled me a couple of bouncers. But I think the Australians quickly got to grips with the fact that the more they got at me the better I played. I was just a young free spirit, playing fearless cricket and watching the ball not the man.

I ended up getting after Jason Gillespie in particular. He didn't hit his lengths as well as he'd have wanted to and didn't get in as many yorkers as he'd have planned. I'm not sure it had any impact on how he performed in the Test series, though: I was just hitting it sweet and the straight boundaries at Bristol are incredibly short so I got a couple away. Then, in the forty-sixth over, I smashed him for a six and two fours, which pretty much guaranteed the win, and I finished on 91 not out.

I've heard that, in the dressing room after the game, I said, 'Not bad, am I?' The truth is, I really don't remember, so I don't know if it's true. I do know myself, though, and I'm sure there have been times when I've sounded arrogant in saying things like that, but actually it's been totally tongue in cheek, taking the piss. I do it with my buddies all the time: if we're on the golf course and I play a good shot, it'll be all 'Oh, I should be on the tour . . . ' But sometimes people like to perceive things in a certain way because it agrees with what they already think, and there's not much you can do about it.

On Fast Bowling

Fast bowling is one of the most entertaining aspects of cricket, a joy and a thrill to watch. For me as a fan, that's great. But for me as a batter, I'm not going to let anyone run in and dictate. If someone wants to be aggressive with a ball that's really short, I can get out of the way. If it's fuller, I just tap it to fine leg and face him from the other side. And if I see either delivery early, they're getting whacked for four or six.

I look at short-pitched bowling as if I'm in a boxing match. I can either be the fighter being hammered, against the ropes with my head back and not looking at what I'm doing, just trying to cover up. Or I can be like the very best fighters, pressing forward and dominating. So that's what I try to do. It's about getting your head at the ball, being fleet-footed and attacking from a good, strong base. And because there'll be only two men back, sometimes just a fine leg, I see it as a good scoring opportunity.

There are two main reasons I've never struggled with chin music. One is that determination to be positive, and the other is that my eyes have always been pretty good. Partly, that's just who and how I am, but I've also worked bloody hard to make it work for me.

Growing up in South Africa and wanting to be a cricketer, I knew that I'd need to be comfortable against bouncers – and I also knew that Hansie wasn't. So I invented a drill called rapid-fire, which involved getting a guy to stand halfway down the wicket in a shed, or even on turf, and have six balls ready to throw at me. I've always practised with six balls because there are six balls in an over – I never train without six balls, and if you're going to throw to me you've got to have six balls in your hand.

I'd take guard and say, right, knock my head off. Then I'd stand there and whoever it was would throw the first ball straight at me, *poom*, or a bouncer, *poom*, and I'd try to hit it, but the second would be coming at me already and then the third and the fourth, *poom, poom, poom*, and I'd either hit it, get out of the way, or get hit – sometimes on the head.

The more I practised, the better my eyes got, and the more confident I became; I started getting into better positions and playing more shots. And if I'm not getting hit from eleven yards, I'm definitely not getting hit from twenty-two yards, so had no reason to be scared out in the middle. Train hard, play easy.

But you also need to be able to trust your defence when your stumps are under attack. If you can't play a bowler's best ball, then you've got issues. Basically, you're screwed.

Again, the answer is to drill as hard as possible. That way, when the speeds get up to 90 mph – the point at which you don't have time to tell yourself what to do – you can rely on your instinct to take over.

You train your brain to respond in the right way, because sometimes, when your mouth's dry and your heart's racing, you can't control what you do. That's why guys play shots that they don't want to be playing – they're ticking, and they've not done the kind of practice that controls those emotions.

It's hard to explain the buzz of facing serious pace, of a strong, fit, athletic guy sprinting in and hurling a ball at you as hard and as fast as he can. I'd call it a true experience of instinct – that's the best way of describing it. People talk about instinct, but what is it? How can you describe being instinctive? Well, when it comes to fast bowling, instinctive is when your blood fizzes and boils, not in an angry way but in excitement, your muscles tighten up and you have that element of fear which makes you do things that you can't normally do. Which makes you jump out of your bubble to a place that you don't want to be, but go to anyway. It's like when you're chased and you run faster than you thought you possibly could. Instinct, in the form of self-preservation, takes over.

When I think about the quickest bowling that I've faced, three men and three scenarios come to mind: Brett Lee at the Oval in 2005, Shoaib Akhtar in Pakistan in 2005 and Fidel Edwards in the Caribbean in 2009. They were all up at around 95 mph – which gives you 0.47 seconds to react – but there were still significant differences between them.

Lee gives you the ball, and by that I mean he has a beautiful action, allowing you a perfect view of what he's doing. What was especially tough about handling him on that day was the pressure of the situation, and it was that which took me to another place.

On the other hand, when Akhtar and Edwards run in their hands are all over the place and that makes them much harder to play, especially for a ball-watcher like me. I'm sure the coaching manual would tell them to do things differently, but if I was working with a bowler my advice would be to keep things as untidy as possible.

Shoaib and Fidel are also both slingy in their action, which means that even though there's a seven-inch height difference between them they're quite similar to face. Unlike Morné Morkel, for example, whose height and straight arm mean really short short deliveries that are relatively easy to duck under, theirs are quite full and don't get up as high, so always feel like they're skidding right into your throat.

What was special about Shoaib was the theatre he created. He's a real fun-loving guy and a good performer, so he'd whip up the crowd to create massive excitement and expectation whenever he came on, just by the fuss he made about getting ready. Then he'd be smiling and smirking at the batters, using his own ego and bravado to play on theirs. Did they have the balls to confront him? Could he tempt them to confront him?

They knew what everybody in the ground knew: Shoaib was going to sprint in, hair flying, nostrils flaring, to bowl as fast as humanly possible. And the Pakistani people were proud of that. They had this superfast superhero who delivered spells that were just incredibly fierce.

Shoaib himself was absolutely obsessed with the pace that he generated. When he bowled that 100 mph rock to Nick Knight in Cape Town during the 2003 World Cup, he seemed happier than when he got a wicket. He just loved being known as the fastest bowler in the world, though he had a very good slower delivery too, which made him even more difficult to face and got him a load of success in that 2005 series.

Likewise his action, which made it pretty much impossible to track the ball. His arms started by his sides and waved everywhere in the run-up; then, as he approached the crease, he'd go so deep into his load-up that the actual delivery came at you from behind his back. While that was happening, his arm would hyperextend at the elbow and bend the wrong way, in towards his body, which meant that as it came over his shoulder for release there was a kind of whipping sling effect as it snapped back into place.

But if Akhtar was all about the speed, Edwards was running in to hurt me. He's a great guy. The last couple of years, we've played together for St Lucia Zouks, and he's said, boy, I knocked your head off and gave you serious licks in 2009, and he did, I felt it. Goodness, I got a lot of runs in that series and I batted for a long time, but I hardly faced a pitched-up ball from him; he wasn't at all interested in pitching it up.

Basically, that was the West Indies' way of combating sides – going after their main dangerman, whoever that was at the time. Fidel would bowl his fastest stuff whenever I happened to be on strike, rather than in particular spells.

In that situation, all you can do is rely on the technique you've built over a number of years. For me, it's getting into the trigger position early and not moving my feet much – or, against the very fastest, not moving my feet at all, just moving my head.

You have to try to put the danger out of your mind, but at the same time you can't ignore it. So you tell yourself you're in a battle, then try to stay calm, trust your ability and enjoy it. I absolutely loved the challenge and loved the fight, that's why I play. I'm a competitor and I'm a winner, and though I want to win the game most of all, I also want to win the individual contests.

It's funny, because I'm not at all interested in jumping off bridges attached to a piece of elastic, or jumping out of planes attached to some nylon, but I wish I'd been around to face Curtly Ambrose and Courtney Walsh. I guess I see the point of that, and feel like I've developed a defence mechanism to combat the danger.

To be clear, though, I'm not suggesting that I love it when they bounce me. Nobody likes fast bowling at their head, especially when it's for a long period of time.

But I also see it as a scoring opportunity. I think, okay, they've taken out lbw, bowled, caught behind. If I can get my bat on it, I can get off strike because it's going to go down to fine leg, and if I get it, if I see it, I can hit him for four. I've always thought that if someone's attacking me like that I need to attack them, so it's always going to be an exciting passage of play.

What I'll do is watch the bowler's action for clues as to what's going to happen – but I'll always be careful. It's dangerous to start guessing where fearsome deliveries are going to go because you stop focusing on what you're good at and what you're supposed to be doing – you're not reacting any more. You get onto the back foot instead of worrying about getting onto the front foot, and you're planning to play your shot when you should be looking for and tracking the ball. If Shoaib Akhtar was running in and bowling at 95 mph, I never said, right, I'm going to hit this through cover. No chance.

Against Australia in 2013, Trotty started doing that kind of thing. What happened was that Mitchell Johnson roughed him in up the home one-day series, and when that happens the opposition start talking about it, they target you, you start to struggle and it rocks you to your foundations. It becomes more of a mental battle than a technical one, and when you add that to the fatigue of a guy who has obsessive focus and never gets a break, you've got a problem.

Johnson was bowling brilliantly, though. He'd always been talented – we'd seen that at Perth in 2010 – but he was inconsistent. He'd obviously done a lot of work with a psychologist on his mental power, and Dennis Lillee had helped him with his bowling. He didn't spray the ball anywhere near as much as in previous series, and there was also a lot more structure about what he did: he was clear in what he wanted to produce, which was very short, very fast, very straight deliveries.

We all spotted that things were different in those ODIs. I remember opening the batting and thinking, Goodness there's a new beast here. The ball's hitting the bat a lot harder and he's got a lot more control.

I'm not sure if the selectors thought he wasn't ready for the Test series, or if they deliberately held him back for the Australia leg, but picking Johnson for the limited overs was definitely a good way of putting the fear of anything into us before we even arrived down under. We didn't know exactly what we were in for, but we knew we were in for something.

Mentally, I prepared by getting myself into a zone where I knew he was going to be at me, which meant a lot of rapid-fire. I didn't see others train tough like that – and I'm not quite sure why they didn't – but people do whatever works for them.

Where my English cricketing career began: lining up for Nottinghamshire at Trent Bridge, aged twenty-two

Playing for Natal against England's touring team in 1999. My four wickets included three England captains – Atherton, Hussein and Vaughan!

White Lightning: Allan Donald, warpaint on and in full flow against India in 1991

Hansie Cronje in action at one of my favourite tracks, the Oval, in 1998

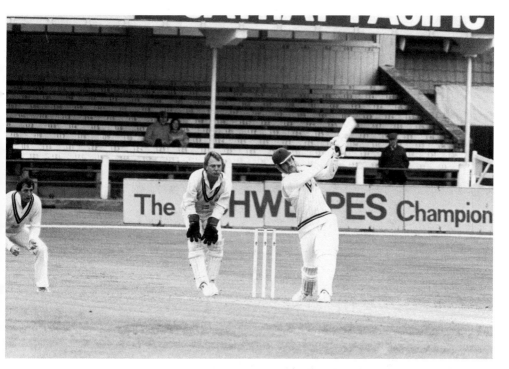

Clive Rice – a much-loved
and greatly missed mentor
of mine – batting (with Paul
Downton keeping wicket) at
Trent Bridge in 1983

Another great coach,
Graham Ford of Surrey

The first flamingo, at Edgbaston in 2008. I didn't see this as the invention of a
new shot, just a way of manipulating the field and getting some runs

And the switch hit, against Scott Styris at Durham in 2008

Practice is everything: at the Oval (*above*) in 2007, and (*below*) at the
2010 Cricket World Cup

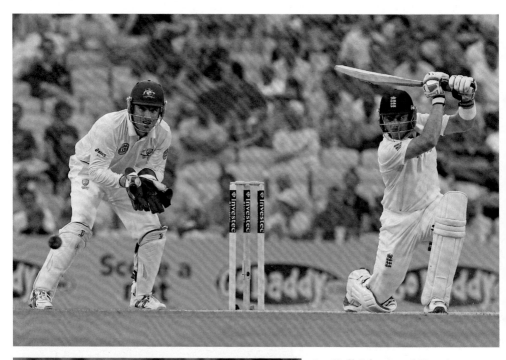

Ian Bell (*above*) and Damien Martyn (*left*), the two most elegant batters of my era

George Bailey takes a brilliant catch at short leg off the bowling of Ryan Harris, ending my final innings of the 2013/14 Ashes

In the zone: hitting a six on the way to 355 not out vs Leicestershire at the Oval in May 2015

Celebrating my century at the Oval on the final day of the 2005 Ashes series. Luckily Gilo was there to remind me we still had a job to do

That said, I don't only prepare for bouncers. I can't be so worried about bouncers that my stumps go out, that's just stupid, and you never get six of them in an over. So I'd make sure there'd be some full balls in there for me to look after – after all, I'm always looking to come forward. And I was always asking myself one important question: have I done enough preparation to go and be successful in this series?

In the first innings of the first Test we all saw how quick Johnson was and how much Trott was hating it – he was caught behind on the stroke of lunch. I was in next, so during the break I took Mushtaq Ahmed to the nets and got him to bounce me with wet tennis balls. I was thinking, shit! If this is happening to Trotty, what am I going to do about it?

Out in the middle, I get ready to face, and as soon as Johnson starts running in I can see that he's coming faster than before, real aggressive, and he's got great rhythm in his action, huge forearms pumping tight like he's in a fight. With me. He's a very athletic, strong bloke, who gets a lot of power in his load-up and delivery stride, and I'm doing my usual, just watching the ball, though it's hard because his hands move a lot.

Then, when it arrives, I realise that it's not as fast as Trotty's made it look. That's partly because of the practice I've done and the confidence it's given me, but also because I'm in a different kind of mental space to him – not as worried, upset or emotionally fatigued. I do have my knee issues, but otherwise, I'm okay.

Even so, I don't play the first ball especially well,

knocking it into the leg side, and his second confirms that I'm facing a new bowler – it's clocked at 91 mph. Not as fast as Lee in 2005, but it feels faster, because of the left-arm angle into the body and that little bit of extra zip that you get off the wicket in Australia. So there's even less time to play the shot, which means that I need to move faster and be holding my position earlier. It's a very difficult proposition.

I start talking. I say, Mitchell, you care more about being whacked around the park by me today than I care about losing my wicket to you. I'm trying to make him think, I'm in a bit of a battle here, because he knows it's true. He has confidence issues, I don't, and I've never had an issue with getting out, I've never been scared of getting out. Never.

It makes no difference. In previous series he'd send the ball down the leg side or wherever, so we weren't really fearful of him because there'd always be a scoring opportunity on the way. Now, he's on me the whole time, and so are the fielders at leg gully and short leg. He's bowling an off-stump line, his bouncer's on top of the stumps too, and that slingy action means it's never too short and it's always well-directed, flying up at my neck – he's using it to set me up by going short, short, short, then trying to knock my stumps out with a quicker, fuller one. But he hardly ever comes too full. His change-up ball is a good length, which means he can nick me off, he can get me caught at short leg, and he can for sure make me do something that I don't really want to do. He did that a lot, to everyone, and it was not pleasant. Mitchell Johnson destroyed us.

Michael Clarke also used him really well, in short spells – four overs, three overs, two overs. It was good captaincy, resisting the temptation to keep him on for longer, however well he was bowling. Generating pace like that takes a lot out of you, so it was important to keep him fresh, and he was, every single time. I can still see it now, Johnson bounding into the wicket, aggression and meaning and purpose in every delivery. The only consolation was that you knew you didn't have to survive too long before he was off, which is why I tried to leave as many balls as possible and not bother hooking him – though at Brisbane, that was how I got out in the second innings.

Obviously we spoke in the dressing room about how he'd changed his game, how mentally stable he was, and how he'd changed his whole psyche. But mainly it was about how good he was and how quick he was. Our tail-enders, Broad, Swann and Anderson, were absolutely petrified, and it's not hard to see why.

Not that you could blame them. This was probably the fastest bowling they'd ever faced, and there just aren't many fast bowlers around these days, let alone fast left-armers. And the way that our number three played at the Gabba sent shockwaves through the whole batting order, with everyone thinking, jeez, if he's the rock and he's been our rock for a number of years and this is happening to him, what the hell's going to happen to us?

We got battered in Brisbane and then lost the toss in Adelaide. People say that if we'd won it, things might have been different – it's not easy going out there after fielding for two days, let alone to face Johnson, who's super-fresh because of all the rest he's been getting.

But the wicket was still the same, and it didn't change that much either; Johnson just performed so well. The way he knocked over Cook, an extremely good player of pace, first innings for 1, second innings for 3 – man, he was very, very fast.

In the second innings of the fourth Test I decide to fuck with him again. I'm thinking that I know how well he's bowling, I'm batting well and want to take him to a place he doesn't want to be, to try to mess with his rhythm. He's easily Australia's biggest threat, and I know from previous confrontations that he can be easy to rile.

So I keep stopping him as he's running in, and he's shouting at me: what the fuck are you pulling away for? Stop fucking pulling away! I explain that there's a kid by the sightscreen, that I can't help it, and tell him I won't bat until I'm ready. Then there's a piece of paper flying around, so I decide to make an issue of it, and he loses his rag again.

But after that, he just goes back to his mark and gets on with it, showing again why he's the boss of this series – eventually he bowls me for 71 and gives me a proper send-off. Clearly, he's improved as a person and improved as a cricketer, which from his perspective is good to see; off the field, he's a nice guy. But from an Englishman's perspective, it's just more bad news.

Perhaps the only slight weakness in Johnson's make-up is that he doesn't really swing the ball, which I think is because his whippy action stops him getting his wrist into as good a position as some others. That means that if you can line him up you can leave a lot of balls – unlike with Mitchell Starc who, even when he's bowling badly, attacks the stumps and has that inswinging yorker to clean people up.

We saw that in the first Test of the 2015 Ashes, when Starc got seven wickets and Johnson only two. But he was able to bounce back on a dead track at Lord's: because he's got a really strong shoulder he can generate the missing pace himself.

If Johnson can get his wrist right, and conditions are favourable, then you're in a lot of trouble because all of a sudden he's attacking your stumps with the inswinger and all forms of dismissal are in the game. It happened to us at Perth in 2010, when he got four top-order wickets – one of them mine – in a single spell, then two more pretty soon afterwards, and we were all out for 187. It was an incredible performance.

But you can't really talk about Johnson without talking about the magnificent Ryan Harris, a stock bowler and a strike bowler in one. Johnson's numbers are way better when Harris played too, because of the pressure he created at the other end – in the same way Colly and I presented different challenges for the bowlers, they did the same for batters. Harris used to give you even fewer scoring options than Johnson, which is why our top order were far more bothered by him. He aimed for the top of off stump, but fast, with swing and reverse swing, hit the bat hard, forced you to drive and did it through long spells. The challenge was to find a way of keeping things moving even off his good balls, so that he knew he was in a contest.

Even though, after the 2013/14 Ashes, Johnson went to South Africa and destroyed them, when it came to the deciding Test in Cape Town it was Harris who was the main man. He knocked over Smith, Amla and Duminy in the first innings, and then with time running out in the second, first he got de Villiers, and then Steyn and Morkel, the last two wickets.

It's obviously a shame he's had to retire, while Johnson, though he's still good, has cooled down a little too. When India toured Australia in 2014/15, Virat Kohli scored four centuries and one fifty in four Tests – he's got quick enough eyes to pick deliveries early and quick enough hands to play shots, as well as that rare combination of touch and power.

But it's also because of his method. Virat's aggressive, and much as Johnson is aggressive too, he's still insecure. If you look to score off his bad balls, and there actually are some – he didn't send down many against us – he's not the same proposition. In that series, Virat played some magnificent cricket strokes, as did Murali Vijay and Ajinkya Rahane – they're all bloody good batters.

Virat's a much better player now than he was when he came to England in 2014 and averaged 13.40. Those hard times toughen you up mentally, and it was good for him to learn about failure. It makes you a better person, it makes you understand that life's not always rosy; it just makes you. It also means that you appreciate success, so that when you go through a purple patch and get the opportunity to nail runs you make it count.

The closest I got to a series like Virat's in Australia was probably when South Africa toured in 2008: I made two tons and a 94. Still, the innings against them that most people remember came in 2012.

The first Test was at the Oval, and I played nicely in the first innings until Kallis got me caught behind pulling for 42. Then, I took guard in the second and realised that I might as well have been holding a hockey stick. It was just one of those horrendous days when I felt rubbish.

I wasn't sure how I'd go when we moved to Headingley. Though South Africa were lacking a top-class spinner their pace attack of Morkel, Steyn and Philander was absolutely superb, which is why none of us scored against them consistently.

For me, Morkel was the trickiest to face. Obviously it's the pace he's got, but others have that; what they don't have is the angle. Not only does he slant the ball into you, but because he's so tall the bounce from back of a length is constantly attacking your ribs. You can't enjoy that.

And, like Harris did for Johnson, he gets wickets at the other end for Steyn and Philander, who both have better numbers than him. Philander's a good bowler with a nice wobble-seam delivery, but he's no Morné Morkel. Morkel's problem, though, is that he doesn't hit or threaten the stumps as much as the other two. Most of the time his deliveries are bouncing over the top, which eliminates lbws and bowleds as a means of dismissal and is why 162 of his 218 Test wickets have been caught. But then his mates take advantage of that with fuller lengths, and that's how the best attacks work: they have variety, which stops batters from ever feeling comfortable.

The other thing about Morné – and like Chris Tremlett, in fact – is he's such a nice guy, such a lovely human being, and that doesn't help his bowling. At six foot five he should be running in aggressively and knocking people's heads off, but he doesn't command the same fear as Johnson, or Steyn when he gets the red mist. If Morkel had Steyn's head – holy shit – he would be the worst bowler in the world to face, but that's just not who he is.

Steyn, on the other hand, has the image: a proper snorting fast bowler whose incredible numbers in the subcontinent show you just what a great he is. He always tries to swing the ball, get it up to the bat and get you caught at slip, and his short ball is very, very short. But, like Brett Lee, he has a beautiful action that lets you see exactly what he's up to, so he's someone I've always loved facing.

It's funny with Steyn, because he actually bowls better with the old ball than the new ball. It doesn't come through as fast, so he has to put a lot more into it – he's not just running in and getting through his action at 82, 83 mph. So

96

his pace cranks up, and feels quicker still when he's reverse-swinging it. Maybe it's just perception, because of how late the movement is and how much you're thinking, I need to be on my game here, but some bowlers do seem to find an extra yard when the onus is on them to make things happen.

Before the second Test in 2012 the South Africans were talking about really attacking me with short stuff. I'd heard it in the media, but Jacques Kallis also said, yeah, I'll bounce you out again, and one of the others told me, we're coming for you properly – we're going to get you again. I knew it was banter, but I also knew that I needed to pay attention.

So when we got to Leeds, I just practised short balls. I didn't do rapid-fire because the wickets weren't quick enough to make that worthwhile, but I did spend time in the nets with Graham Gooch throwing at me with the claw – all the batters did, really.

Even so, on the first morning, I wasn't feeling especially great. But then I was walking off the field after the warm-up and Mike Haysman, the South African commentator, came over. You like this sort of wicket, don't you? he said. So I asked what he meant, and he told me: you average eighty every single time you bat here.

That filled me with confidence and I immediately started to think of all the good stuff, instead of thinking about how they were going to get me out, how I felt last week and all the short-pitched bowling I was going to face. I told myself, that's right, I've got hundreds here. I got a big hundred here against Yorkshire, I got a hundred against Pakistan, a double hundred against the West Indies, and suddenly I was full of confidence and belief: I knew that this was a good place.

South Africa made 419 in their first innings, so when I went in at 85–2 we were under pressure. And I was under pressure too, from things off the field.

But once I walk over the ropes, that's it – now I'm only interested in how I'm going to pick up the bat, and I pick up the bat beautifully. I take guard and feel great. I think something's going to happen.

Steyn's first delivery to me is a bouncer; I get out of the way easily, miss the fuller one that comes next, and that's me down the other end. I'm watching the ball nicely, saying to myself, I'm away, I'm good, I'm all good.

Trotty faces all of the next over from Morkel, and then Steyn's back. He bowls two short ones in a row; I pull one for four and glove one for four, and that's it: I'm on, I know I'm on. I'm going to score runs.

I get to 16 and they bring on Imran Tahir, so I crash his first ball through extra cover to the fence. Then Trott whacks him too but gets out to Steyn; Bell comes in and hits Tahir for six, so they take him off and I go back to hitting the bad balls as they come. Bell goes just before tea, and James Taylor comes in.

Soon after we come back on, I hit Steyn for four in consecutive overs. The second one gets me to my fifty, a single takes me down the other end and Taylor plays out the rest of the over.

Morkel's arranging himself a field – third man, deep fine leg, square leg, deep square leg, midwicket and cow corner – and then announces that he's coming around the wicket, as if I couldn't tell. We both know that he's saying, I'm coming at you. If you want to take me on, you should. And I thought, well, I will take you on, because I'm not scared of losing this battle. I'll baseball you out of the attack.

First go, I pick out the fielder at midwicket; on the second I push towards Amla at short leg and he doesn't react quickly enough to hold it. Big mistake, because I only need two sighters. The third ball I absolutely hammer through midwicket for four, the fourth to cow corner for four, then I get off strike with a single and they decide that's that tactic done.

Too late – I'm there. Steyn bowls the next over and I cover-drive him right away, then slash his third delivery over point. I've gone from 52 to 69 just like that, and I also punish Kallis when they bring him on.

I'm on 95 when the second new ball becomes available, and they take it right away. I smack Philander's second delivery through the off side for four, dab the next one into the on side, and that's my century.

Everything comes back. Making a hundred is a big emotional release in any circumstance, but my wife's here, which makes it even more special. As I race down the wicket, I do a running jump and skip, swish my bat, take my helmet off, kiss my bat and point to Jess.

Steyn comes back at the other end, and it's quiet for a bit, but then I start rushing again. Because I've played against him a lot, I've noticed that when he runs in in rhythm he's looking for shape and swing, and when he runs up faster he's going to bowl a short ball – I guess because he's an emotional guy, and taking the aggressive option makes him act more aggressively. So I always try to anticipate what's coming before he delivers, and this time I know that he's going fuller. As soon as he's in his delivery stride I lunge onto the front foot, and that gets me into the perfect position to whack straight back at him on the up, making him take cover. It's a pretty good feeling.

Then, in his next over, I'm watching him charge towards the crease, thinking, short ball, short ball, short ball . . . right, get in position to play the short ball, trigger, normal trigger movement.

As it leaves his hand I see it early, I see it slowly, I pick the length early and I know where it's going. Normally, my hands come towards the ball from on top of the stumps, but because I've anticipated what's going to happen, this time they're already in position outside them, and I play a sort of half-cross-batted shot, a sort of pick-up shot with a half-closed face, that times the ball through midwicket.

I can describe what I did now, but at the time I wasn't quite sure – something that also happened, in different circumstances, during the Oval ODI in 2005. I ran at Jason Gillespie expecting a full delivery, he came short and, thanks to a good wicket, quick hands and the ball in the right area, I sent it into the stands, baseball-style. It wasn't something that I practised, and I've never done it again, it just happened in the moment.

I always watch the replay after a play-and-miss to see what went wrong, and after a boundary to boost my confidence – and there's Steyn's face on the big screen as he walked back to his mark, saying, what a shot that was!

I know that Dale doesn't like bowling to me because I've always gone well against him, but that's a definite tick in my box in terms of the contest we're having today. Of course, he's one of the greatest bowlers in the world, but I have my methods against him just like I had my methods against Shane Warne, and I've just played the best shot of my career.

Afterwards, 149 not out overnight, I went back into the dressing room. Emotionally, I've no idea how I managed to do what I did out there – I just feel free when I'm batting, and I certainly felt free during that innings.

Back at the hotel, I went to my room full of joy and elation and just cruised – I have never been one of those players to look in the mirror and think, yeah, fair play, that wasn't bad. And, thanks to Sachin Tendulkar, I don't watch the highlights either.

When we played India at Nottingham in 2007, the two of us chatted during a rain break about form, pressure and the weight of expectation. I asked whether he read the papers, and he said, no, why should I read tomorrow what somebody's got to tell me about what happened today, when I know exactly what happened today?

I was interested, so wondered if he was so strict when he'd got a hundred or two hundred.

No, I still don't read that stuff because even if it's the most amazing article, there will be one line in there that is negative, and that line is where the human nature in you takes over and thinks, why did you have to write that?

Immediately, I realised that he was right, because I remembered a time I'd hit a ball to midwicket on 98, gone through for two and not pushed for a third. The next day I saw an article that was very complimentary about how well I'd batted, but criticised me for celebrating and not taking that extra run. And all I could think was, you bastard. I've just scored a hundred for my country and all you can do is pull me up. I knew it was just one line, just a throwaway comment, and that's why it proved Sachin's point: human nature means you can't help being bothered by tiny negative stuff you know you should ignore.

So, chilling in Leeds, I had room service and went to bed – but it took me ages to drop off, and then I woke up early. Even though I'm a big sleeper, it's always like that after a hundred.

The next morning I was out to Morné second ball. It's incredible how often that happens to me, starting again and failing, whether I'd made a score already or not. We were all aware of it in the dressing room – Prior and Trotty used to comment on it, and so did Straussy, because he was another one who really didn't go well the day after.

This time I'd even told Tim Bresnan that he'd better be ready, but I hoped I was joking. I told myself to be positive, that I was on 0, that it was the same attack I'd nailed yesterday – all that stuff. But it made no difference, and it was annoying. Even if it's in my nature, or human nature, to concentrate harder when it's most important, it was still my responsibility to get myself back in and I didn't.

And that was how I finished the Test: annoyed. We pushed hard for the win, ended up with a draw, and my innings was worth nothing. Personal success is cool, but if it doesn't happen for the team you're still left with a hollow feeling.

On Medium-Pace Bowling

Fast-medium bowlers are often harder to face than the real fast guys. Hovering around 85 mph, they're still quick enough to put you on the back foot, and a lot of the time have more accuracy, control and variation. They can defeat you with simple pace, but because of the seam and swing, also have other ways of beating you.

The best pace bowler I've faced is Mohammad Asif, the only man quicker off the ground than through the air. Somehow the ball always seemed to accelerate after it pitched, probably because he almost always hit the rope to make it shoot off the track – it was his wobble-seam delivery that Jimmy Anderson copied after seeing it in 2010.

You just can't play that kind of movement, that natural variation of the wicket, because it happens so late – and that's why it's a bowler's best friend. All you can do is hope you react quickly enough to cope, but Asif's length was so full you had even less time to defend than usual.

What you can try to do is stop it happening in the first place. I generally try to nullify the seaming ball by standing outside my crease, so that I can get to it before it does anything. Plus, I won't be out lbw, because I'm either not in line or too far down the pitch, and I won't be out bowled, because I'm not missing with both my bat and my pad.

But like every plan I made against Asif, it didn't really work; in this case, for two reasons. The first was that he was also swinging the ball, movement you need to play later, not earlier – even if you know which way it's going, which I didn't. And the other thing was that even though he was only bowling at low-to-mid-80s, he had a very quick bouncer that was very hard to pick, meaning I couldn't just lunge onto the front foot.

So it was a pretty fierce combination that he had going on there, which is why I wasn't the only one who found him especially difficult. I know, for example, that Amla and Kallis did too, and there's not much they struggle with.

One thing that may have been significant is that, even though I've got hundreds against them, I was never in good form when I faced Pakistan. But even if it's a part of why I found Asif so tough, it's still only a part – he was just a legend.

Even though he only got me out a couple of times,

because he pinned me down and worked me over I would give my wicket away to whoever was at the other end. And I never dominated him, or felt in control against him; I don't think there's anyone else I can say that about.

Another bowler I had trouble with, but for completely different reasons, was Peter Siddle. In seventeen Tests, he's knocked me over me ten times; next best are Brett Lee and Murali with six each, a total Sids managed in the 2013 calendar year.

When I first started playing against him, Siddle was quicker than he was in the back-to-back series of 2013/14, and more of a strike bowler. I don't know whether it's his vegan diet, or just that he had to change his game once they got Mitchell Johnson taking wickets and going for runs, but for whatever reason his pace subsided. He was high 80s and ended up at to low-to-mid, when really, given what he does, that extra gas was important.

Yet he kept getting me out. His role in the attack was to build pressure by bowling maidens, because Johnson and Harris were wicket-takers, but things don't always work that way. I saw Siddle as the kind of guy I should be scoring off and, I guess, had to be scoring off, when really I should have paid him more attention than I did and looked to score more against the others.

Every single time I went out to bat against him and said, right, you're not getting out to Siddle today, respect his bowling, I didn't get out to him. But every single time I walked out there thinking, I'm here to score runs. Where can I hit you? I need to drive this ball, I'd nick off or hole out. That was obviously a massive frustration.

The more a bowler does well against you, the more you start to worry about him, the more you try to figure him out. The more we played against Siddle, the more we realised it was a patience game, so we needed to get on with him that way – which is probably why he didn't get me out after the first innings in Perth.

Those back-to-back series worked out very well for Australia, who were at home for the last five Tests, but not for us. We were mentally drained and physically exhausted. Jimmy Anderson had already proved that he could take wickets on their pitches, and under normal circumstances you wouldn't see a freak like him getting punished like that.

Even though the system stole the start of his career by messing with his action – imagine how good his numbers would be if they hadn't – he developed into an outstanding bowler. He has an incredible ability to find and control shape, deceive batsmen with his variations and be consistent enough with his lines to execute a plan.

He's been the best in English conditions for a long time, and with experience got so much better abroad, keeping the ball in the right areas and throwing in the leg cutter and the wobble seam when necessary. The thing that really sets him apart, though, is his use of reverse swing.

Reverse swing is not only harder to bowl than conventional swing – it's a real art – but also harder to face. It doesn't happen all the time, so you can't prepare for it; it happens in conditions where the ball's already skidding a little bit, and – most importantly – it happens late.

I first heard about it when Wasim Akram and Waqar Younis were playing, but didn't face any until 2005, when Brett Lee was getting deliveries to tail. My plan is usually to leave as many as possible, and those that I can't leave play as late as possible, after the swing.

Another thing I like to do is stand leg side of the ball, opening up my stumps to give my bat a clear pathway to defend them. That way there's no chance I'll be out lbw, and because I can negate the inswinger and away-swinger by hitting freely through the line, there's also less chance I'll be out bowled. If I miss it I miss it, if I nick it I nick it, but I'm giving myself the best opportunity to play it confidently because I'm in position to play the best shot. That means it'll take something seriously good to get rid of me.

The best reverse-swing bowler I faced was Zaheer Khan, a brilliantly skilled operator – you need to be to survive on the subcontinent, where conventional swing doesn't last long. His pace was up at 85, 86 mph and he was a left-armer who could move it away from you or send down a big hooping in-ducker – but, more importantly, he was dextrous enough to hide the old ball without sacrificing any pace. It meant you had no idea what was coming, so your technique had to be good once you found out. While it's true that I only got out to him a couple of times, when he was on I always knew that I was in a contest.

Similar to Zaheer was Chaminda Vaas: not quick, but quick enough. He could land the ball in the same area again and again with the kind of control you see in a high-quality spinner, and with enough movement to keep you honest. Unlike a lot of left-armers, he was always attacking your stumps, which meant that you had to line him up properly. I used to open my stance a little bit to play him straight back from where he came, or to mid-on.

What Vaas didn't have, though, was that ability to hide the ball. Other than Zaheer, the guy I've seen do that best is Anderson, who also loses nothing from his pace or action. In terms of skill, Jimmy is phenomenal, with such great wrist control – just an absolute master.

England's greatest reverse-swing bowler, however, was Darren Gough, and probably our greatest-ever death bowler as well. He was consistent in his lines, clever in his lengths and also got real late movement. But what gives him the edge over Jimmy was his height, or lack of it. Being short meant that he could get the ball to skid, and because it was rarely bouncing over the top the stumps were always under attack, which forced batters to play a lot more than they wanted to.

Reverse swing also gives you balance, especially if you don't have a spinner who's a reliable wicket-taker. In 2005, Freddie and Simon Jones were dangerous with the old ball, so we could use Gilo for control, but even later on when we had Swann, because Anderson, Broad and Bresnan, our three other regulars, all got it to tail, there was always a threat from both ends.

When you have units like that you can start to put plans together, and in our 2011 team that became number one in the world, it was Anderson who took charge of the process. He was the leader of our attack, a responsibility given to him by Andrew Strauss as a way of getting the best out of him – what it said was, you're our main guy, we trust you – take responsibility.

But it also told the others that he was somebody they should look up to, somebody they could talk to about their game, who'd had success in all conditions and delivers on the big stage; that's why Alastair Cook asked him to stay with the team even after he got injured during the 2015 Ashes. The leader of the attack is basically the confidence-giver, and not just to the bowlers: batters know you need twenty wickets to win a Test, and that getting them is much harder than scoring enough runs.

Another impressive thing about Anderson is how good he is at getting the best batters out. Look at Kumar Sangakkara, an all-round great who doesn't have too many weaknesses – Jimmy's knocked him over seven times, more than any other bowler, and only once more at home than away.

In Sri Lanka it's always ridiculously hot; it's a war of attrition. Sangakkara would spend a couple of sessions just defending and playing straight, because he knew that, at the end of the day, when the overseas bowlers were absolutely shattered he'd dominate them.

We targeted his off stump to nick him off early, and we'd also bowl full of a length if we felt that his feet weren't moving on a particular day – or before they got going. Amazingly, the plans came together in 2012, when in both Galle and Colombo Jimmy got him for first-innings first-ballers, caught behind and caught at slip.

In terms of how he'd bat through a day in the subcontinent, Mahela Jayawardene was very similar. A beautiful touch player with amazing finesse, he was incredibly hard to bowl to. But in England he struggled, and we went for the outside half of his bat, looking to hit the top of his stumps, and it worked pretty well. Taller bowlers, like Broad, Freddie and Liam Plunkett, did well against him, as well as Jimmy, obviously.

A little like the two great Sri Lankans, the three great Indians – Sachin Tendulkar, Rahul Dravid and V. V. S. Laxman – would play great innings, long innings, but they would never take the game away from you. I'm told that, before my time, Sachin was an assassin, but when I played against him we always felt we had a chance.

He's another Jimmy dismissed more than anyone else: nine times in fourteen games, five at home, four away. He'd swing the ball away from him, then shape it back in, because we thought he was a strong lbw candidate, and we'd also look to draw him forward onto the drive to nick him off. Then, if he got in, we'd target his stumps and try a few high bouncers, because once the ball's above the eyeline you've never got proper control of it, and all the more so given how heavy Sachin's bat was. But mainly, he just left those.

Dravid, though, was just The Wall, an absolute rock, and he got loads of runs against us. Nothing we tried – and we tried everything – worked in England, and nothing worked in India either. I found him more technically sound than Sachin, more defensively solid, but not as good at attacking. Sachin had the ability to hit some incredible shots and make you feel like your bowling was insignificant, whereas Dravid made you feel like your defence, when you batted, was insignificant compared to his. His sheer brilliance at making bowlers go, where the hell do I bowl now, because I can't get through this bloke? was just phenomenal, whereas Sachin would make you think, what happened there? because he's just hit your fast bowler's best ball through extra cover or whacked a spinner through midwicket.

I guess it's not much of a surprise that Jimmy also had success against Laxman. He was a guy we knew we could play the patience game with, which is perfect for a bowler with discipline and control. Obviously it's not as simple as saying that a batter of Laxman's quality should probably have got a lot more hundreds, because concentration is one of the skills you need to get them, but he would get in and get out, instead of making you pay. You always knew that you were in the game against VVS – even on his day he'd give you a chance, and he scored a few fifties against us but never a century. So it was just a case of trying to create pressure, waiting for the opportunity and then grabbing it.

Graeme Smith, on the other hand, cashed in big against us. Technically, he'll say the same thing about his method that I say about mine: we don't look like the best players in the world, but the positions we get our heads and our hands into when we strike the ball are strong positions. And his mental toughness more than made up for any glitches in his style – he was so strong at the crease, and had such presence, which is why he got the numbers he did.

The flaws were still there, though, so we tried our best to exploit them. The way that his bat came through angled towards leg side, and the way that he was so dominant in that area, meant that his timing needed to be perfect.

We'd look to bowl on off stump, full of a length and swinging back into the stumps. That way, if he missed it, it was out, and there was also the chance that he'd be so eager to play into the leg side that we'd drag him across and get him lbw falling over. Matthew Hoggard, the leader of our attack before Jimmy, had big success with this in 2004/5, and it was something we always remembered.

But if you talk about executing a plan, then the man who stands above them all is Glenn McGrath, a seam rather than a swing bowler with an amazing ability to dig a trench on a length, right on off stump. His Hawk-Eye and pitch maps were just phenomenal, and those groupings were the key to his success.

And there really wasn't much variety: he just ran in, hit

his spot and made you play. I think he managed it because he had such a strong, tall action – a perfect action – that also helped him hit the bat hard, at a really good pace.

As a batter, your off stump is your guideline. If you know where it is, you're batting well, and if you don't, you're going to struggle. So when somebody attacks it day in, day out, it's disconcerting. You can't leave anything, you're worried about three modes of dismissal – the nick, the lbw and the bowled – and you're wondering when you can attack.

My method for playing McGrath was to walk down the wicket, looking to disturb his length by meeting him where he pitched the ball and where he felt comfortable. That forced him to drag it back and give me more scoring opportunities on the back foot, and then, when he came fuller again, looking for lbws, I could hit him down the ground or through midwicket.

It's true that I faced him at the end of his career, when, although he was at his craftiest, his bouncer wasn't as dangerous, but I'd have done the same whenever we met. Otherwise, it would have been him dictating.

Of course, being tall made it easier for me to get forward, but I still think that was the way for everyone to play him; when he devastated us at Lord's in 2005, that's what I was telling all the guys at the other end. It was a good spell, don't get me wrong – Richie Benaud said it was one of the best he'd ever seen McGrath bowl, and he should know – but it wasn't unstoppable, and I didn't find it that hard to face.

The problem was, the other guys just didn't have the confidence to do what I did. McGrath had already got Vaughan and Trescothick out a few times in their careers, and it just wasn't in their nature to walk at a bowler, it wasn't in their make-up. But it was in mine. I was young and I was confident, so I did it.

On Spin Bowling

S pin bowling is a great tool and a great weapon. In the first innings, it's mainly used to dry up an end, to build pressure through maidens and to let the quicker bowlers have a break. And then, in the third and fourth innings, once the wicket's deteriorated, it's there to win you the game.

But it's not quite as straightforward as that any more. I think we're seeing the death of the conventional spinner, and in the not too distant future mystery spin will dominate. By that, I mean spin that turns either way – leg spin, basically, because it's almost impossible to bowl the doosra legally.

The problem for the off-spinner is that he's predictable. Guys play so much more positively now, and they're confident in anticipating what's coming; bats are big enough to force against the turn, even mis-hits can go for six. So, without the variation of a ball that goes the other way, you might be fine to start with, but eventually you're going to struggle.

That's why I found Shane Warne so much easier to play than Muttiah Muralitharan, even before T20 changed everything. Murali spun it both ways, and if you didn't pick him you'd come unstuck, whereas Warne hardly ever bowled the googly, because it was too hard on his shoulder. So I never had to think, he can knock me over with the wrong'un. I really have to wait for the ball.

Instead, it was the leg-spinner, the top-spinner, the flipper and the zooter. Obviously, the leg-spinner turns from leg to off, and the top-spinner dips faster and shorter than you'd expect, then bounces higher – you can pick it because the seam's upright and you can see it rotating over the top of itself.

The zooter is a straight delivery disguised as a leg break, and a delivery Ian Bell really had trouble with. The action seems to be the same for both, but actually, when you look closely, you can see that the zooter comes out the front of the hand, which means that you can pick it. You can also pick it through the air, because it doesn't spin and has a scrambled, ruffled seam, whereas the leggie – even when bowled cross – has perfectly positioned revs. If you don't spot it, you're in trouble: although it has a similar trajectory to the stock ball, it's a lot quicker in flight. You're meant to think that it's a short one, and once you've realised that it's not it's too late, because it skids onto you and either knocks your stumps out or gets you lbw.

The flipper is similar to the zooter, also coming out of the front of the hand, but more obviously – it's snapped with the thumb, index and middle finger. That gives it backspin, which is another way of identifying it from the crease, and when it arrives it's quite a lot quicker than the slider, then pitches shorter and bounces lower before hurrying on.

Warnie being Warnie, all he did was replace the missing googly with bullshit. He'd always be in the media, talking about this new ball he'd been working on; in 2005 it was the slider, which turned out to be the zooter under a different name. But although we all knew it was rubbish, he still ended up taking more wickets in a series than he ever had, and more than everyone else: forty at 19.92. To put that in context, to show just how good it was, Andrew Flintoff, at his physical peak and in the form of his life, was next, with twenty-four at 27.29.

So, even though Warne had less variety when I faced him, I wouldn't say I didn't face him at his best. If it wasn't for Warnie we would have absolutely hammered one of the greatest sides ever, and although a lot of Australians said the same about Freddie, well, if neither Warnie nor Freddie were there, we still would have beaten them. Our players outplayed theirs.

At that point in my career I played spin really badly. I used to stay on the crease, plant my foot and rely on my reach, my hands and my eyes – and when they failed me, I always had my pad. Pre-DRS, no umpire would give me out if I'd got in a big stride, so I was fine, pretty much, however great the bowler.

I was also lucky. Warnie was my captain at Hampshire and we got on great, so I never had the intimidation factor that everyone else did; there was no intimidation at all. Absolutely none. I would just laugh at him, and that helped me a lot. I call him Shaun, Shaun Wayne, so if he was talking to me in the middle, I'd be saying, shut up Shaun, shut up Shaun, whereas if someone like Belly had done that, he'd probably have gone berserk.

He was such a big, vocal figure in the dressing room, just a really respectful, really nice guy. Obviously he's one of those people the media have tried to turn into some kind of beast, but actually, in terms of friendliness and politeness, he's a superstar. You send him a message, he'll always reply to you. He'll always remember names, he'll always guide you, and he'll always talk about the positive things in life. He's never, ever afraid to voice an opinion and he's never, ever afraid to help, wherever and whatever it is.

He's just the kind of person you want to hang around with. You want to know how he goes about his business and what makes him tick. He brings confidence out in you, and makes you want to be wherever he is.

And that was a crucial part of why he was such a great bowler. When I faced him in the nets, I realised straight away that I could pick him, but then, most people could – that wasn't the key with Warnie. It was all about the theatre he created in the middle. He was an absolute performance artist.

The show started when he was told he was coming on. As soon as he took off his hat and gave it to the umpire the crowd got up, and that was when Warnie's juices started flowing. He'd come down the pitch a little, go back and make a big show of wiping his hands on the crease to dry them off. Then he'd spin a few balls to himself, but he'd be looking you in the eye the whole time, reminding you who was in control and building the atmosphere that he wanted in the middle. He'd bowl a few sighters to mid-on and mid-off and eventually walk in after a pause at the top of his mark, still staring at you, gaining momentum closer to the wicket. He had a lot of energy in his delivery stride, and then his arm came over and his wrist gave such a rip that there was this *prrrrh* sound on release, like the fizz you hear when a golfer hits the ball, a kind of whistling vortex. *Prrrrh!*

Whenever I've spoken to Warnie about bowling or heard him speaking about bowling, whenever he coaches youngsters, he's all about spinning the ball as much as possible. Just get those revs on it, because that's what brings the dip, that's what brings the drift and that's what brings the natural variation which messes with the batter. Most of all, that's what gave him the best chance of getting wickets, which was what he was about – he was always looking to get you out. He had no fear of failure, he always looked for the positive option, and he was willing to risk a six for a wicket.

And that's what a lot of players are like, the great players. You look at them when the pressure's on and you just think, that guy wants to be there, he wants the confrontation. He's desperate to be involved in the confrontation.

There was Murali the silent, smiling assassin; Ricky Ponting, the aggressive assassin; and Shane Warne, the jovial assassin, who just loved it. A lot of people know what they should do when things heat up, but can't perform because they let situations get to them.

Shane Warne loved them; he got so buzzed by them. Everything about him said to everyone there, this is my time. I'm on here.

But as much as Warnie loved the battle, he also loved the art of battle, and he was brilliant at it because he's a special person as well as a special player. He just understands people and how they work, so had the knack of really zoning in on their vulnerabilities; it was all part of his genius.

Along with the opposing captain, he sometimes targeted the young guys, and in 2005 properly went for Ian Bell, who he called the Sherminator. He'd be telling him he didn't have a clue, asking if he knew where his next run was coming from, saying that I should be ahead of him in the order and, actually, what was he doing in the team anyway? He had everything over Belly in that series, and even though Warne only got him three times, he decimated his confidence for the bowlers at the other end.

Daryll Cullinan was another: a good player who Warne completely wrecked. Then, when Warne started calling Andrew Strauss Daryll in 2005 – just a little thing – it was enough to make Straussy start to wonder.

You had to be very careful not to let him get to you psychologically, because that's what would destroy you – he got so many of his wickets by destroying his opposition. If you weren't mentally strong he'd get right on top of you and nail you to the ground, whether it was by standing at slip abusing you, running from slip to slip at the end of the over and telling you how bad you were as he went past, going on about how easy it was to knock you over, or loudly discussing all your technical faults in front of you. He always found a way.

Warnie was a great reader of a newspaper. He always used to read the news. So if a player was under pressure and the media were on him, he'd always be able to bring up an article that was in the *Telegraph* or the *Sun* or whatever to have a go at him. The guy's just an outstanding piss-taker.

He also had an amazing ability to put you under pressure when you weren't actually under any pressure. If I hit a beautiful shot, if I slog-swept him for six, he'd still create a scene. He'd be shouting '*Oooooooh!*' like he was *that* close to getting me out. Aw, mate, you don't want to miss that! Which made me think, oh my gosh, jeez, was I almost out there? Yet I'd just smashed him into the stands!

And all this is loud enough for the umpire to hear, so he

thinks there's a wicket on the way as well. Then Warnie would start talking to the batter, but for everyone's benefit: Dead, mate. If you'd missed that . . . That was dead! Dead! Then he'd look directly over at his man behind the stumps and he'd say it again. Dead! Stone dead!

Then the umpire would nod or whatever and that would be job done: he knew this was Shane Warne, and that Shane Warne was bowling a line that could get someone lbw. And somehow, even though he knew it was all bullshit, because he's this amazingly confident person Warnie kind of believed in it himself.

Other times, he didn't get a decision he wanted, and when that happened he'd be right at the umpire. He'd turn like he was shocked, and say, 'What do you mean? What? Aw, mate. *Aw!*' Then there'd be deep sighs, like he was really hurt, and then he'd start again. 'How is that missing? How is that missing?' By this time he'd need to get back to his mark, so on the way he'd say, 'Mate, if he misses another one like that you can't let him off again. You *can't* let him off twice. What are you trying to do to me?' Warnie would just be in his ear the whole time, so the non-striker was getting it too, and if that's you, you know that if you're up the other end next time there's a shout he's going up again with more chance of getting the decision, which makes you more wary of making a mistake.

It's funny, because if you speak to Warne now he'll talk about how many wickets he'd get playing with DRS. But I always tell him he'd have got fewer, because of how many decisions he got thanks to spinning the umpire round his little finger. He just has this charisma, this infectious personality, that encourages people to agree with him, especially on the cricket pitch.

It wasn't just the batters and umpires who were caught up in it all. When Warne was bowling, his teammates knew they could get a wicket every single delivery, so the enthusiasm just went up 10, 20 per cent. The chatter around the bat changed as well; everyone was at it. It was just a really good phase of the game when he was involved.

Warnie had his tricks with the ball too. When you're lining up a spinner from your stance, you know that anything coming down and tracking between your eyes is probably pitching in line with the stumps, but you've got a decent chance of hitting through it to play a solid defensive shot.

On the other hand, as soon as the ball's outside your eyeline you've got to move your head to follow it – only a minor change, but one that makes hitting it just that bit trickier. So if you were getting to Warnie on the stumps and banging him through midwicket or down the ground, he'd bowl a big looping leg-spinner well outside off stump. And because you were on top, as soon as you saw a little bit more air you'd think, I'm going to go at him here. But that was exactly what he wanted. The delivery would turn so far that, if it pitched, it would be a wide; his plan was that it didn't, because the temptation not to miss out dragged you right over to play a big, silly shot when you couldn't really see what you were doing, and you ended up caught at point, caught at slip, or knocking the ball straight up in the air.

None of this works, though, without the bowling to back it up. Everyone knew Warnie had it, and no one could pretend that he didn't.

In 2005, the plan against him was to be positive, to try to score and to try as hard as possible not to let him just bowl; we knew that if we let him get into a rhythm he would knock us over. There were no other tactics, because every individual has their own method – Strauss was a sweeper and played the ball into the leg side; Trescothick hit down the ground and slog-swept well; Vaughan used his feet and hit wonderful cover drives; Freddie was a straight power hitter. Warnie was always going to get wickets, but if we ignored his hullaballoo and attacked him in the meantime, then at least we were still adding to the total. Our left-handers played him really well at the start of the Edgbaston Test, Vaughany was brilliant at Old Trafford, Freddie got him at Trent Bridge and Gilo and I did nicely at the Oval.

But at Adelaide the following year we forgot all of that, and were punished with one of Warne's most miraculous performances. Batting first, we'd declared on 551 then bowled them out for 513, and at the end of day four, we were 59–1 – the game was headed for a draw.

Next morning, we were in trouble pretty quickly. In the first twelve overs we only added eleven runs and lost both

Strauss and Bell, so when I came in we were 70–3. In the first innings I'd batted really well against Warnie for my 158 and forced him to bowl around the wicket – always a victory, which immediately made me think, 'Negative ploy'. Because Warne's a great believer in being positive all the time, he'd claim that he was still attacking the stumps by bowling into the rough, but that was just more bullshit.

Every now and again he'd get people out doing that, and there'd be the occasional delivery that ripped back in, but really, it meant you'd pushed him off his preferred line, so he was just trying to dry up the runs. Without the googly, every single ball pitched outside leg stump so I could get my pad in the way with no fear of lbw, he hardly had a caught behind, and he definitely didn't have a bowled – I don't think I've ever got out to a right-arm spinner coming around.

But he tried it twice – briefly when I was in the 30s, and then again when I was in the 90s, for half an hour or so. It was actually pretty strange, because it turned me versus Warne into a pretty boring stage of the game; I was just padding up, padding up, padding up. Eventually the crowd started booing, but I wasn't about to give it away, especially because I'd always said to him, oh, you'll never bowl me around my legs, never.

Then, on that fifth morning, I'm 2 not out and it happens. He's coming at me from over the wicket and pitches his first ball on leg stump. I wish I'd been playing the reverse sweep at the time – I should've been against any leggie or slow left-armer – but I hadn't practised it enough, so wasn't very good at it. Instead, I play a real dumb, lazy shot, a sweep that's meant to get me off strike. I miss, it spins big and I'm gone, bowled around my legs. It was stupidity, that's all: me taking it for granted that I could just knock him around the corner. I couldn't, and that was that.

Even so, we should still have left Adelaide with a draw, but the guys just went into their shells. We were sitting on the balcony watching nervously, because we could see that the runs were going nowhere and the Aussies were starting to get a little bit of a taste of it. Brett Lee was running in bowling fast reverse swing, no one was picking it, and everyone found it really difficult to play.

Then, from the other end, there was Warne, creating an atmosphere and getting the crowd involved. It was very clever how he did it. Occasionally, he'd bowl one into the rough so it spun miles, or a real wide ball that pitched on fourth, fifth stump – slow, but also a big spinner. You didn't go after them because you knew they were nowhere near anything, but they still put some doubt into your mind because you knew turn was there for him. And when the crowd saw how much, and then again on the replay, there'd be a big 'Whooooaaaah!' They'd be even more behind their team, and the atmosphere became even more intense.

Back in the middle, Warnie would be talking to himself. Aw, I just need to get that straight. Aw, if I get that straight! he'd be saying. And then he'd laugh as he was walking back past the non-striker and stop for a word with the umpire: don't forget I've also got the straight one. You've seen my straight one today, you saw it the ball before. Just remember I've still got the straight one.

That day in Adelaide, his bowling was picture-perfect. The ball was pitching leg stump and spinning, he was getting beautiful drift and the zooters were out too, creating pressure and opportunities. He just had so much control.

The big thing that makes playing spin in Australia different from anywhere else in the world is the bounce. It brings in more modes of dismissal – the nick to slip, the bat–pad – and it's also good for the batter because it helps you hit through the line of the ball; the beautiful balance of cricket, really. But even when Warnie tossed up a few to entice the drive, nothing. So in an hour and a half we went nowhere, when all we needed was maybe another sixty, seventy, maximum eighty runs. And as good as it was, there's no bowling so good you can't score off it.

The problem was that we didn't play with proper intensity, Paul Collingwood and Geraint Jones especially; Gilo, meanwhile, was just too wary of Warne and knew that within a few balls he'd be gone. So there were no aggressive shots, which is why Colly finished 22 not out off 119 deliveries. What he should have done is used his feet more, and instead of defending half-volleys, pushed them.

Because we played so negatively, the Aussies sensed weakness and took wickets regularly, through poor shots, through pressure that they created and through good bowling – Warne even got his googly out to get rid ofdHoggard. Basically, we were thinking, draw, draw, draw, but they, and Warne in particular, were shouting win, win, win, win! We just capitulated.

I know that all over the UK people thought, this is a draw, I can go to bed, then woke up in horror, thinking, what the fuck's going on? Don't worry, we were the same in the dressing room.

Of all the spinners I played, the only one who could compare to Warne was Murali – he got the ball to do the most, and he had this calm confidence that he could knock you over at any given stage. What made him hard to face was the pace at which he bowled, especially at the start of your innings; once you were in and less vulnerable, he'd look to vary it a bit more. But his trajectory always stayed flat – there was never much flight or drift – so you had to decide what he'd sent down and what you were going to do about it much more quickly than normal.

I tried to pick him through the air. Ideally, you'd do it from the hand, but with him I couldn't – anyone who says they could is lying. Off the surface was too late. I looked at the rotation of the ball.

Obviously his wrist position was different on release: the off-spinner came marginally out the front of his hand, and the doosra out the back, basically like he was giving a bacon slice. But it was impossible to see that from the other end, because of how quickly he did it and because the ball was camouflaged by his hand. Unlike with some others, though, I never doubted the legality of his action. He was just a biological freak with an amazing, flexible wrist, and that was how he generated so much speed.

Playing Murali was like playing fast bowling, like playing bouncers. In the same way that I know instinctively whether to duck, whether to pull or whether to get out of the way, my instinct saw those rotations and told me where I needed to defend and where I could hit the ball. But because you could never be sure, I never felt in control.

The only clue he gave was in his line. The off-spinner pitched outside off and looked for off-stump, and the wrong'un pitched on middle, middle and leg, either to straighten or, if it was the doosra, to spin to slip. And because you knew that he was always attacking your stumps and that every ball would turn big, the doosra could never be the off-spinner, because if it was, it would rip straight to leg-slip or 45.

Two balls, bowled beautifully – that was all it was. People said he also had a top-spinner, but if he did I certainly didn't notice.

The first time I played against him, in the summer of 2006, I did pretty well. In the first innings of the first Test at Lord's I made 158, though when I was on 52 Farveez Maharoof had me caught off a no ball – I guess you shouldn't bowl those.

Murali was actually down on his pace that day, because it was the only way he could extract any spin – the pitch was so true he'd just have skidded onto the bat otherwise. That got him three wickets, but our scorecard tells you the pitch still won: Trescothick 106, Strauss 48, Cook 89, Collingwood 57, Flintoff 33 not out.

Even so, I could see what he was capable of, and the sweeps I used were nervous cross-batters to get the score moving. But in the end, it was laziness that did for me: I tried to knock Chaminda Vaas into the leg side while standing tall with my head in a horrendous position, played right across my front pad and missed. We then bowled them out for nothing; they were much better following on and the match was drawn.

Something that surprised me in that game, and which I never really got, was how defensive Murali was with his fields. From the start he had his mid-on back, he'd have a cow corner and a deep square leg, then a short leg, midwicket, backward point, extra cover, mid-off – and obviously he'd have a slip. He hardly ever had two men catching around the bat, which I thought was strange, especially for a bowler of his magnitude. He should have had a short leg and a silly point every time.

Then, as soon as I'd whacked him a couple of times, he put everybody back on the boundary, even though I was playing release shots, not shots of great control, power or precision. I was just thinking, jeez, I don't know which way this ball's going here, let me play a cross-batted sweep and then it doesn't matter, I can force it hard enough that it'll go.

After that, I had to be a bit more circumspect, but there

was a lot less pressure because the boundary riders meant I could always get off strike. If I'd had Murali's skill I'd have believed in it enough to say, if you want to hit me for five fours go on then, I don't mind. But he preferred to go for ones and twos, and he was like that even when the pitch gave him more help.

In the next Test, at Edgbaston, we skittled Sri Lanka for 141, then Murali took six wickets as I made 142 out of 295 – the next-highest scores were Vaas and Strauss's 30s. I'm not quite sure how it happened, because the pitch was an absolute road and beautifully paced for strokemaking, but what really helped me was my reach. I could stretch out to balls that the others would have to be defending and punch them through the covers, either playing on top of the bounce or on the bounce, to turn a good length into a half-volley.

The main thing, though, was my head position, which was excellent. There was one lovely delivery that Vaas bowled on about off stump, and I drove down the ground for four only just past the stumps on his side. That told me I was playing in very, very straight lines.

So I scored pretty quickly, getting boundaries on both sides of the wicket – I was in and it was one of my days. Then, because they'd shut down the other end, they decided they'd try and do the same to me. Jayawardene, the captain, and Maharoof, the bowler, obviously got together and said, we need to cut out his scoring. We're getting wickets around him, and if we stop him scoring we might be able to get him out.

They decided to bowl wide outside off stump with seven men on the off side, putting a deep square-leg and a mid-on on the leg side just for security. Because I played with a straight not a cross bat I always favoured the leg side, and on that occasion I had the pace of the wicket. So, wanting to manipulate the field and get some runs, I walked across my stumps, put weight on my left leg, which was quite far over, and kind of pivoted on it to pull my body right around, playing through mid-on. Maybe it looked risky, but I didn't see it that way at all, because of that straight bat. It was the first flamingo shot.

It's nice now that people remember it and it's got a name, but at the time I just saw it as four. I thought, right, you've put all the men on the off side and you're bowling all the way out there, now you're going to have to start bringing some back and bowling a little bit straighter. And they did. Two flamingos made them send a man over, and my next two boundaries came through the gap that created at extra cover.

The other thing about that innings – apart from me getting a boundary down to third man, which I never do – was that it was the first time I played the switch hit. In commentary, Geoffrey Boycott called it a 'reverse-thump, not a sweep', and maybe that's a reason why people think that they saw it first when Scott Styris bowled to me in an ODI in 2008. But that was just when I got hold of it best – I'd also used it in the 2007 World T20.

I hadn't specifically planned to bring the shot out that day, but obviously I was feeling confident, 136 not out and whacking the ball in areas where I wanted to whack the ball. I'd been playing it in the nets for a while, trying to see if it worked as a scoring option and just having some fun, and had found that I was never getting out to it.

So when Murali packed the leg-side field – he had to, because he was such a big spinner of the ball and the doosra didn't do as much as the off break – I thought, to hell with it. The off side was my best scoring option, which I used against him a lot – through extra cover, mid-off, wide of mid-off, backward point – so when the opportunity to switch-hit presented itself I took it and it went well.

Sure, I'd have looked a clown if I'd got out, but I just didn't think it was likely: I only ever play the shot in situations where it takes out a couple of modes of dismissal. So not against a left-arm spinner bowling from around the wicket, because he's pitching a lot of the balls on the stumps and trying to hit them, but it's fine against a leg spinner bowling around the wicket or a left-armer coming over, because there's no lbw and there's no bowled. If I've defeated them from their natural angle they're not going to tie me down and make me hit into the leg side where they've got seven fielders; I'm going to change hands and I'm going to whack it the other way.

I first thought of the idea as a kid, playing courtyard cricket with my brothers. If you were out for a golden duck you had to face six balls left-handed, and if you got out again you were out for good. So I thought, I need to become good at this.

I also played a lot of hockey growing up, which gave me good wrists, and playing tennis and squash, I never had any hassle on the backhand – it was always an easy shot for me, and an aggressive shot. I honed my timing because I used it a lot, the backhand cross-court, the backhand volley, the backhand slice drop shot, and that's what the switch hit is: a backhand. You swap the position of your hands on the handle of the bat, so for me the right moves to the top and the left to the bottom, but the left is just there for stability – the right does all the work, just like it does in a racket sport.

After the Styris game, there was a lot of noise about the switch hit – something I'd never even considered for a second. It's similar to my 158 at the Oval, I guess, in that I didn't think I'd become well known because of it – I just played. I don't rate myself or see myself as a famous person, I just see myself as a sportsman with a familiar face. All I'm doing is trying to get the best out of myself and have as much fun as possible.

It also never occurred to me that no one had ever played the shot before, nor that anyone could even think about having a problem with it. So when the MCC decided to have a meeting to discuss whether it was legal, all I could think was, don't be so stupid, I'm a right-hander batting left-handed. What's the problem? I'd rather bowl to somebody batting the wrong way round than have them bat the right way round. Ridiculous.

I only survived one more ball before Murali got me, and he took four more wickets in our second innings, which gave us a scare. But we went on to win, which made my knock one that gave me a lot of pleasure. It's always nice to know that I've contributed in a tough environment, but for it really to mean something the team has to win.

The final game of the series was at Trent Bridge, which was a complete and utter dustbowl. I was actually talking to Sangakkara about it recently, and he said that when they turned up and saw the pitch, they couldn't believe it. So they checked with the groundsman that the one it looked like we'd be playing on was the one we'd be playing on. He confirmed it, and all they could say was, wow. They just knew that Murali was going to roll us, and he did: three wickets in the first innings, eight in the second and they got away with a 1–1 draw. I remember the ball turning prodigiously, but mainly I remember it being the most ridiculous track ever prepared to play against a subcontinental team in England, let alone one with an all-time great spinner who'd go on to become the most successful bowler in the history of Test cricket.

The pitch made even less sense given that Graeme Swann was still two and a half years away from getting picked. We had Monty Panesar, who took five wickets in Sri Lanka's second innings, but it wasn't the same. He did bowl some beautiful spells, and had good control, pace and bounce, but he wasn't a great like Swann. Perhaps he could have been, given more opportunities – it was just that, hard as he worked at them, Monty didn't have much talent when it came to batting and fielding, which was a problem.

Swanny, on the other hand, could hit a bit, catch well and clean people up in the second innings. But the amazing thing about him was his ability to knock them over in the first, not just hold up an end like most spinners. In sixty Tests, he got three wickets or more twenty-five times, four or more seventeen times and five eight times; to show how good that is, Shane Warne's numbers, in 145 Tests, were sixty-six, thirty-eight and eighteen.

The other special thing about Swanny was how successful he was against left-handers – they make up 122 of his 255 Test wickets. Obviously he was helped by the fact that there were a lot of them around, and a hell of a lot by DRS, which got him thirteen referral outs and also allowed umpires to give him more decisions in the first place; of his lefty dismissals, forty-three were lbw, compared with twenty-seven of 133 with righties. But plenty of others played in similar circumstances with results that were nowhere near as good.

With Swanny in the team, we could ask for pitches to suit him, confident that the other team wouldn't be able to compete – as we did in the 2009 Ashes. It didn't work out for him in the first Test at Cardiff – or any of our attack, for that matter – but then at Lord's he got four wickets in the second innings, Freddie got five and we won. After that, Edgbaston was a draw and the Australians dealt with us at Headingley, which meant that it all came down to the final Test at the Oval. On a specially prepared strip, Swanny took four in each innings and we regained the urn.

In the return series, though his second innings five-for at Adelaide helped set up the series win, Swann didn't get too many wickets. But his control meant that our seamers could rotate from the other end and were always fresh when we needed them.

Playing in the subcontinent, having him meant that you could take on India and Sri Lanka at their own game. When we won in Colombo in April 2012, he took ten wickets, and then later in the year, bowled superbly with Monty to help us beat India.

I was captain when Swanny came into the Test team – I gave him his cap. That was also in India, in 2008. I wanted him because I wanted an extra spinner, but he was bowling so well in the nets that I didn't think we had a choice in any case. I'm a pretty good player of the turning ball, but he was making me think – and getting me out, especially between bat and pad.

So at Chennai, once we were in the field, I tried to get him on as soon as possible, because with his loud and boisterous personality, I didn't want him standing around too long, watching and waiting. I wanted him to feel welcome, and because he's quite an impatient guy, to think, I'm in the game here now, I can start doing things. So I threw him the ball for the fourteenth over, the last before tea, and in it – his first in Test cricket – he got both Gautam

Gambhir and Rahul Dravid lbw, and just carried on from there.

Because Swann was always looking to spin the ball, his line to right-handers was outside off stump, attacking both edges. If it turned, he'd be looking for bowled, lbw or the inside edge for bat–pad; if it didn't, he'd nick you off to slip. Or he might toss it up outside off to entice the drive or the prod, but one thing was constant: you would have to be playing, because of how much purchase he was getting.

To left-handers, he'd come around the wicket and attack their stumps. Some balls would spin, some balls wouldn't, and he'd knock them over with lbws and caught behinds.

I'd probably have played him by getting across my stumps, to counteract how much turn there was, and because he didn't have a doosra – Hashim Amla did that very well in 2012. Then I'd look to smother his spin and score against it through the off side, basically defending the good balls and hitting the rest through the covers, or square leg if it was short.

But whoever was facing him, he was super-clever in the way that he read them, and also how he picked a different line, length and pace to bowl on different surfaces. That nous that he had, right from the start of his Test career, came from his experience – you can see the difference now if you look at Moeen Ali, who's learning on the job. Swann was twenty-nine before he played Test cricket, and when I think about my own career the four years between arriving in England and playing international cricket were four years of growing and learning, in which I batted hours and hours for

Nottinghamshire. If I'd been chucked in after one county season I might well have failed.

Because he was so comfortable with his game, Swanny brought a lot of confidence to the crease. Clearly that's part of who he is, but he was also getting a lot of wickets, which must have helped.

Despite that, though, he never spoke to batters; he just went about the art of spin bowling, which for him meant an off-spinner with a half-scrambled seam that he ripped really hard. On release, it made the same *prrrrh* sound that Warnie got, and it gave him a similar kind of natural variation.

Basically, Swanny had two deliveries: the one that spun, and the one that didn't. And, whatever he might say, he had no idea when or why it would go straight on, because he did the same thing every time: just tweaked it as hard as he could.

If he got his action perfectly right, which he usually did, the ball would talk, whether it was first innings or second. And when that happened it gave batters a problem, because they were wondering whether there was going to be spin. One would play for it then ... natural variation, *bang*, lbw; another wouldn't, *bang*, caught behind, caught at slip. It's just what happens when you always give it your all.

Like Warnie says: spin that ball and forget about all the other nonsense. You might not get it right, but it'll hit the shiny side instead of hitting the seam, then natural variation will take over and take it straight on. If the bowler doesn't know what's coming you can be sure the batter doesn't either.

Really, it was just another circumstance in which being positive helped, and it brought both Swanny and the team lots of success, so good on him. He was still a great craftsman, and I certainly don't think any less of him for it.

I guess the other thing to say about Swann is how well Matt Prior kept to him. Prior's a fiery character, an in-your-face, aggressive kind of guy. He really enjoyed the battle in the middle and did a lot of talking behind the stumps, mainly the generic chatter that keepers go through every day to keep themselves occupied: 'Come on lads, top of the stumps', 'Let's get behind the bowler', 'One brings two', 'Our half of the bat', 'Forty-four per cent out lbw', all of that. But he also helped Swanny set his fields, and between them they got the men in the right positions. They had an excellent partnership.

Swann did plenty for Prior too. A lot of keepers are good players of spin because they have to read hands as part of their job – they could spend twenty overs a day looking at rotations of the ball. So when it comes to their batting, they pick deliveries and lengths quicker than anyone else, and it was that, along with his very fast feet, which helped Prior become one of the best players of spin I've ever seen. He really was a very good cricketer, and extremely positive, which meant he could change the momentum of a game quickly.

Especially effective on the off side, Prior was brilliant at manipulating fields and rotating the strike, and never looked in danger. He was our Gilchrist, basically, and I know that our opponents would've had a lot of team meetings about him because they couldn't afford for him to get in. When it came to playing spinners, the Dairylea triangle really was Brie.

But it's Swann who England really miss. Too many of Moeen Ali's wickets come when the batters go after him and miscue, rather than from brilliant deliveries, nor can he hold down an end like Gilo did.

Nathan Lyon, though he's much better and has improved a lot since I last faced him, is similar. Michael Clarke – another great player of spin – always used him very defensively against me. As soon as a fielder came up I'd whack him over the top, and sometimes I'd still do it even if he put the fielder back. Clarke was a smart captain, though, so would have Lyon bowling around the wicket and force me to hit over mid-on, long-on and cow corner, and sometimes I'd get out. But no one's ever thought, oh shit, Lyon's bowling today.

On the other hand, plenty have thought that about facing Anil Kumble. I've played with and against him, and he was a magician, an artist.

Basically, he would bowl wicket-to-wicket top-spinners, building pressure, getting the odd ball to do something. He didn't get huge purchase; the thing with him was his variation of pace, flight and length, and his ability to land the ball on the stumps again and again. He turned the leg break a little and the googly a little more, but it only needs to do a little to get the edge; he'd draw or hurry people into shots and they'd be gone. I doubt there's anyone else who got Langer, Hayden, Ponting, Martyn and Katich – as well as Lee, Gillespie and Bracken – in the same innings, as he did at Sydney in 2004. And of course, he then followed it up by getting four of the six that fell in the next – this time, Hayden, Martyn, Waugh and Gilchrist.

But, great spinner that he was, I never found Kumble that difficult to play. I had more grief from a couple of far lesser spinners when we toured Bangladesh in February and March of 2010. In each of the one-dayers I got out to left-armers, Abdur Razzak and Shakib Al Hasan, twice lbw and all three times for hardly any runs.

Suddenly, there was a huge fuss in the media, people jumping up to dissect the way I played and hoping that they'd identified a weakness. I'd had bad runs before, but I'd never had people say there was something specific that I struggled with.

I knew myself that I had a slight issue. The Decision Review System had come in by then, and so I couldn't just do what I'd been doing, what the likes of Jimmy Adams, Andy Flower and Matthew Hayden had done throughout their careers. I couldn't just get my front foot so far down the track that, even if the ball was straight and hit my pad, no umpire could be sure enough that it would have gone on to hit my stumps. Not any more.

I've always liked and trusted DRS, but it forced me to use my bat more; going forward aimlessly was no good for me –

and neither was staying on the crease. There I was in a nothing position, not a striking position and not a confident position, allowing the bowler to bowl his ball and opening up every method of dismissal to him.

So I had to change. And that was a good thing, because really, I'd been getting away with it all along. It was just tricky to work out, perfect and incorporate into my game while playing a relentless schedule of international cricket.

The fuss then continued into the Tests, where Razzak got me once and Shakib twice. No one bothered to mention that left-arm spinners bowled so many overs in the series that, if you weren't an opener, they were almost all you faced, nor that others got out to them too. Just as it also didn't seem to matter that I made 99, 32, 45 and 74 not out in my four innings, and we won both games.

I then went to the DRS-free haven of the IPL, and spent time picking the brain of the great and gentlemanly Rahul Dravid. Later on, he sent me an email. I've published it before, but it makes sense to do the same again, while we're here:

Champ,
I'll start with a disclaimer: I have not batted against [the Bangladeshi bowlers we had been discussing] and also have not been able to watch any of the cricket in this series. So, if some of what I say makes no sense or is not relevant or practical against these two, just ignore. As we know, giving advice is easy, but until you

have actual experience it's hard to get a real feel of what's the correct way.

They do bowl quicker and if the tracks have been turning then it's always going to be a challenge for anyone.

Against guys who bowled a bit quicker (and I grew up playing Anil) I would look to go forward without committing or planting the front foot. What can happen is we look to go forward which is correct but because we are so keen to get forward and not get trapped on the back foot sometimes you can plant that front foot too early. It sends the timing all wrong and forces your bat to come down too quickly (because once your foot is planted it is a signal for your brain to deliver the bat) resulting in you pushing at it rather than letting it come to you. Also then if it turns you are more liable to follow the ball rather than holding your line and letting it spin past. (Nobody counts how often you get beaten.) Also that results in what we call 'hard hands', which is nothing but pushing out. If your transfer of weight brings your bat down then that's perfect because it always puts the bat in the right place. (I have in fact struggled a bit with that in Aus as my timing has been a bit off and has led to me pushing out at ball and created a gap between bat and pad.) That's the bummer with timing – it's impossible to teach or train.

Anyway, all this stuff is happening in the subconscious and you can't think about it.

You can practise a few things though – in the nets try and pick up length from the bowler's hand, that will force you to watch it closely. Look to go forward but recognise that a lot of scoring opportunities are off the back foot, so while you're looking to go forward you are not committing, the key word is looking, you are ready to rock back and pick up some runs if you can.

One good practice is to bat against Swann and Monty without pads or with just knee pads (maybe not a day before a game!). When you have no pads it will force you, sometimes painfully, to get the bat forward of the pads and will force you to watch the ball. Also the leg will be less keen to push out without any protection. My coach would tell me you should never need pads to play spin!!

KP, you are a really good player, you need to watch the ball and trust yourself. You'll be able to pick up length and line and spin a lot better if you're calm and trusting at the crease. Under stress we miss vital clues especially early on. If you get beaten and it spins past you so what ... you're still in, and realise that you'll pick up the next ball better if you can forget the earlier one. Don't let anyone tell you that you can't play spin, I have seen you and you can!

Anyway, I probably rambled on too much ... all the best, go well!

Rahul

That email was incredibly helpful. I may have been doing what Rahul said when I was playing well, but I definitely wasn't doing it when I wasn't playing well. Sometimes I can be thinking about too many things when I'm batting, or trying to be ultra-aggressive, which was why I was going after the ball too quickly. A lot of English and South African batsmen do that, then rely on their hands and their eyes to play around their pad, but because you can't really move your feet again, you've got to have incredibly good coordination to dominate or score – especially when you're playing guys with googlies and doosras. I was rushing when I should have been waiting, and looking for things that I shouldn't have been looking for.

The problem for me was that we played Bangladesh again at the start of the English summer, so though I made a few more runs again I also got out to slow left-arm again. Then Pakistan, Mohammad Asif and Saeed Ajmal arrived.

I didn't play well at all against them so was dropped from the limited-overs squad, but finally got my form back when we thrashed Australia in Australia in 2010/11. After that, we beat Sri Lanka and whitewashed India, which was great, before we went to Dubai and Abu Dhabi at the start of 2012 for another series against Pakistan.

Our bowlers did a pretty good job out there, but our batters were absolutely done by spin, all of us playing from the crease. We lost 3–0, with Abdur Rehman, another left-armer, and Ajmal in particular bowling really fast and well. Ajmal was mysterious like Murali, and had the ability to turn the ball both ways; tricky at the best of times, very tricky when you're out of form.

But it was actually a good thing that I did badly out there, because it forced me to acknowledge that I hadn't quite sorted things. It wasn't really a specific problem with slow left-arm, though I certainly wasn't at my best when it came from around the wicket and pitched on the stumps. I was just feeling really heavy at the crease and wound myself up about it, which made me go back to Rahul's email to see how and why I was messing up the way I was messing up.

It used to be a thing in the game, or at least in England, not to hit against the spin. But that's rubbish. That's when you're worried about getting out. You want to be in a position that allows you to hit the ball wherever it should go, and to manipulate the fielders to wherever you want them.

Rahul got the better of Swanny in exactly that way in 2011. Playing from the stumps and through the leg side was second nature to him, but anything on or just outside off went through the off side. He could do that because his hands and wrists were amazing, but also because he'd been training his brain since he was a kid; that's what they do in the subcontinent. If you can master playing the ball against the spin, it makes the spinner's job so much harder.

Even though I could do it, I'd always found hitting through the off side less easy and less natural than hitting through the leg side. So I worked hard to improve using my body and technique to stay outside the line of the ball, and even now, for five minutes of every net, I hit every shot through the off side.

Another little thing I started doing when people threw to me was bang every delivery into the ground right at my feet. Obviously, if my bat and pad were down the pitch it was impossible; instead I had to wait for the ball to arrive and play it under my eyes, waiting for so long that if it went any further I'd miss it. That helped me get used to playing as late as possible.

Against spinners, there are two different strike zones. Either you play on the front foot and on the bounce, before the spin – so well in front of the popping crease – or you play on the back foot and after the spin – so right back on the stumps. You decide which to use by picking a length, and only once you know where it's landing do you go all the way forwards or all the way back. I made that easier to do by closing the gap between my legs a little. Suddenly, because I wasn't feeling around my pad any more, there was a lot less chance I'd get out lbw or caught short leg, and because I had options the pressure was on the bowler. If I got him on the front foot and he dragged his length back, I could jump back and get that as well, so the patch in which he could land and not get whacked was very small.

Mainly, though, I was trying to get myself feeling comfortable walking out to face slow bowlers. I needed to know that I had a defence good enough to deal with whatever they sent down, regardless of which arm they bowled it with.

In that Pakistan Test series I didn't feel that way because I wasn't tracking the ball properly. But, amazingly, after a few practice sessions really honing some drill work it suddenly clicked for me in the one-dayers; I waited, picked length and then went.

Because of that, I averaged 93.66, with two hundreds and two Man of the Match awards – Cooky, who'd worked really hard on similar things, got Man of the Series – and in the T20 I got one Man of the Match and Man of the Series. Then, at Colombo six weeks later, I scored 151 against Sri Lanka and the slow left-arm of Rangana Herath.

It's funny how it works. It's just such a little thing, being patient, and you're only talking about a split-second. But it determines whether you're in form or whether you're out of form, and it's hard to do without understanding your game and being experienced enough to know how quickly things can change.

When things like that happen they remind me of a phrase I like to use: 'the art of batting'. I love the art of batting, I love learning how to bat and I love how my game can keep evolving.

And yet, even then, I wasn't finished with left-arm hassle. After all that 'reintegration' garbage, I was picked to go to India in November 2012 and would be on show again. I guess I was used to that, and I knew it was going to be a fun tour. I felt confident in my ability to score because I've always felt comfortable in Indian conditions, and thanks to the IPL I also had plenty of buddies around.

In the first warm-up game, Yuvraj Singh got me out, caught and bowled for 23 – not great. I did get a hundred after that against Haryana, but they were probably the worst opposition I've ever faced in those circumstances. I knew I was playing reasonably, but I also knew I wasn't playing as well as I could or should have been because I was back to thinking my defence against the spinners wasn't particularly special.

The first Test was in Ahmedabad, where India won the toss and made 521–8, declaring towards the end of the second day. We then lost three quick wickets, one of them Trott's nightwatchman, and after he went out and got out I joined Cook for the last two overs before stumps.

That was fine, but taking guard the following morning I didn't know which end of the bat I was holding. The wicket was a slow turner, both of their spinners were on and I realised that I didn't have the confidence to keep out their best deliveries. That made me very loose and frenetic with my foot movements – I was running at the ball – and Pragyan Ojha clean-bowled me for 17 when I was slow to play, then did the same in the second innings when I premeditated a sweep and missed. It was a horrible five days for us, and we were absolutely battered.

The talk in the team was simple: we had to do better. We wanted to win the series, not lose 4–0 like India had to us. Cook, Prior and Swanny had done well, but the rest of us just hadn't.

My baptism of fire, in the 2005 ODI series against South Africa – the most intimidating
environment I'd ever played in

The 2010 World T20 final against Australia in the Caribbean. Ryan Sidebottom (*above*) was magnificent; then celebrating as Colly takes us to a seven-wicket victory

At the crease with Ravi Bopara – a properly gifted player – during the 2009 World T20 Super Eights

Darren Gough taking on Zimbabwe during my first ODI series in 2004

T20 tournaments are playing an important part in bringing fans to the game. Attempting another unconventional shot for the St Lucia Zouks in 2014 (*above*), and having a bowl for the Delhi Daredevils in 2012 (*left*)

Not only does the Big Bash offer a great opportunity to play at some of the world's most iconic grounds outside the hostile environment of the Ashes, it's also a great academy for younger guys to learn from some of the game's more experienced players. Playing for Melbourne Stars vs Perth Scorchers at the MCG in 2015 (*above*), and celebrating victory against Sydney Thunder in the same tournament with twenty-four-year-old Peter Handscomb (*right*)

Freddie celebrating his five-for at Lord's during the 2009 Ashes. One of the greatest players I've ever played with for England

Dale Steyn – a proper snorting fast bowler – putting the England batsmen through their paces at Durham in 2008

One of the most talented fast bowlers of his generation, at his most devastating. Mitchell Johnson at the MCG in the fourth Test of the 2013/14 Ashes

My own career bowling highlight, on the fourth day of the second Test at Adelaide in 2010. Having scored 227, I then got the wicket of Michael Clarke with the last ball of the day

While were still in Ahmedabad I explained to Mushtaq Ahmed what I was doing wrong, and we spent hours together in the nets – I kept saying to him, we've got to get this right for Mumbai, we've got to get this right for Mumbai. He was throwing lots of off-spinners at me with the occasional leg-spinner, and I was on the balls of my feet like a boxer, focusing on picking length and waiting to hit every single delivery through the off side – against the spin, but playing it, not smothering it.

I felt like I was getting into a rhythm and then, as soon as I arrived in Mumbai, I knew that I was. There's a lot more bounce in the pitch and the training wickets there, so everything happens faster: I didn't need to wait as long for the ball or hit it as hard when it arrived. I could play through the line, I could get down the track and chip over mid-off, or I could nip back towards my stumps and punch through backward point.

I read Rahul's email yet again and thought, oh my gosh! And then I thought, okay, if I can work out my defence, if I can get myself playing well here in a couple of days of practice, then I think I stand a good chance.

At the start of the tour I'd been training quantity, not quality. What you do needs to be specific; it's not just about making it tough, but making sure that it's right. I had to say to myself, Pragyan Ojha, Harbhajan Singh, Ashwin, Zaheer Khan – they are going to be my bowlers. What are they going to do to try to get me out?

I knew that Zaheer would be after reverse swing because

the shine on the new ball goes so quickly, and I was batting at four. I also knew that he'd be setting straight fields, so I needed to work out what positions to get into to hit around that, and then practise them.

I was pretty sure that Ojha's left-arm line would be straight, aiming to trap me lbw or have me caught at slip. To eliminate that I had to wait for the ball and show how comfortably I could play him every single time. So I got Monty Panesar to bowl over after over after over to me in the nets, and I made sure I got to the point where I found it easy to bash him wherever I wanted.

Harbhajan would be looking for bowleds and edges, pitching outside off and spinning it back in, so I wanted to defend as I want to defend all spinners: by playing two areas and not getting stuck on the crease. But I also planned to attack him, because from experience I knew he didn't like it.

I felt more or less the same about Ashwin, though he also has the carrom ball, which is similar to a zooter. It's flicked out the front of the hand by the middle finger and thumb, and straightens as it spins.

So I asked Swanny and some net bowlers to help me, and got them to go through their variations. Whatever they sent down I'd defend for five balls, attack for five, play extra-cover drives for five, then sweep for five balls, just going through a full range of shots. I felt ready.

Again, India won the toss and batted, but this time we bowled them out for 327, which wasn't bad. We started our reply quite well, but then lost two quick wickets, so when

I walked out to the middle at 68–2 I'd not really had much time to think about my innings.

It turned out that everything was simple for me. It wasn't a case of worrying, it was just standing over my bat, picking up my bat and feeling totally at ease as I took guard. Ojha had got Trott with the last ball of an over, so after Cook had taken a single I faced Harbhajan. Normally I'm a drop-and-run guy, a dasher, but he pitched a real good one outside off stump and I was able to reach out and square-drive him through point for four. It was something I'd done in the nets, and it was in my zone; one of those where you see it, then you hit it. I knew right there and then that my feet were good.

As I relaxed and built my innings I discovered that I had a proper defence on me, and I was also able to attack. Not only was I moving my feet well, but there was so much turn out there that the bowlers' margin for error was tiny.

What I did really well was not follow the ball once it had pitched. I committed to my shots, held my shape and never, ever let my hands get away from me. That allowed me to score pretty easily. I took the aerial options when I needed to take aerial options, I got back and across to cut, I went down the ground and I manipulated the field with little sweep shots.

Between overs, Cooky and I were constantly telling each other to pick length and play the line, and eventually he got to his century – his fourth in four Tests since becoming captain. No one had ever done that before, and he went on to make it five in Kolkata.

I was on 91 at the time, and when I got to 97, I told him, mate, I'm getting a hundred here. I'm going to reverse. He just laughed and said, you do what you do, you play the way you play.

However it may have seemed, I never had an issue with Cooky, never. Even now, I still don't have an issue. Obviously I didn't enjoy that he was there when I was sacked. I think that he was led to believe that I was somebody I wasn't, that I was causing trouble in the dressing room when I wasn't. But he's a superstar. I've always been positive about the runs that he's scored, I always appreciated that he encouraged me to do what I did and I think he appreciated that I helped win games for him.

So I reverse-swept my way to my ton, but for some reason my celebration was pretty restrained. The first few centuries I scored, the first one especially, I was just over the moon, telling myself, wow, I've got a Test hundred. Then the next few were exactly the same, and when I came up against really good opposition I pretty much went mental: my second hundred against Murali, hundreds against Warne, the one in Colombo, that one against South Africa at Headingley – hundreds against proper bowling attacks in difficult situations. But this time I just didn't feel like it, and I've no idea why.

Shortly afterwards Cook went for 122, ending a partnership that had added 206 off 318 balls. I just carried on, though, and felt like I could predict deliveries, which happens very rarely. Ojha was bowling a leg-stump line with his mid-off up; I knew that he was going to stray, and that when he did I'd be there waiting to club him over extra cover for six. Sure enough, that's what happened, which is why my bat moved so slowly through the shot; it joined the slap off Steyn as the best I've ever played.

Ojha eventually got me for 186 off 233 balls, including twenty fours and four sixes, and not that long afterwards we were all out for 413. Monty and Swanny then bowled India out between them, and we won by ten wickets.

Since then, people have said some really nice things about my innings, that it was the best hundred ever scored by a foreigner on Indian soil. That's very flattering, but also very hard to believe. Obviously, I know that it was good, but at the end of the day the ball was spinning that much that even if I played and missed, I was fine.

Still, I felt like I'd finally sorted my problem for good.

On Form and the Zone

Bad form is mental, not technical – once the mental side isn't right you start making technical errors. It's that negative mindset you can get yourself into, which has you thinking about your game instead of being carefree.

Bad form is worrying. Worrying about your place, worrying about your shot selection. Worrying about what the bowler's going to do and how you're going to face him, instead of working out where you're going to hit him.

One of my greatest strengths is thinking I can score off anyone. But when I've been through patches of bad form, I've thought, I wonder how I'll get out ... jeez, he's a good bowler. What if he spins one past my bat? Oh no, what if my feet aren't moving? Are my feet moving?

What happens is that you'll be playing fine, then you

might waste a few starts, get a couple of great balls, a bad decision, an amazing catch, and suddenly you're concerned. You're there to score runs, you aren't, and your mind's saying, oh no, the rub of the green's not with me at the moment, this is a bit of a bad patch for me.

Then, because of everything that's flying round your head, you stop keeping things simple, you stop doing what made you successful. You're thinking about bad form, you're thinking about what could happen if you lose your job. You're thinking about so many bad things.

So it becomes a battle with yourself. Not technically, because you can still play a cover drive in the nets and you can still whack a ball in the nets, but mentally. Out in the middle you know you've only got the one chance, you're not confident, and as soon as you lose your confidence in sport you're finished.

If you think positively, you play positively. That makes you take positive options, and if you take positive options it's surprising how many times they work for you. If you think about something going wrong, if you think about getting out, if you choose to defend when you should attack, it's amazing how many times that hurts you. Tell yourself what to do, not what not to do – and then do it like you mean it.

Easier said than done. It's very hard to escape the game, especially when it's not going well. I find I have a lot of dreams about cricket, good and bad – the one I have most often is not padding up quickly enough when I'm in next, we lose a wicket and I can't get out there. Classic anxiety, basically.

And when you're out of form, it's on you the whole time. I remember going to bed at night thinking, that's a good attack they've got, fuck, what happens if I don't get my leg across, if my feet aren't moving? What happens if he bowls me a bouncer and I glove it? I mean, he's swinging it at pace – what happens if I'm not in line? These are the kind of things you're thinking, not, I know how to build an innings, hit to mid-off ...

Once you eventually get to sleep you find yourself waking up in the middle of the night worrying about your game. You go for a piss and you're thinking, what can I do when I wake up tomorrow? Or am I just in a nightmare, where I'm in such bad form? Then, in the morning, the first thing you think about is your bad form. You're worried, and not just about batting but your whole life. There are a lot of things that go with bad form, way beyond not getting runs.

That's because so much of who are you are is to do with cricket. It helps you feel good about yourself, it gives you so much pleasure and satisfaction, and it's how you provide for your family. They support you and they're relying on you.

If you're struggling in the international game, you'll be stressing about how your career's going to go and what it will be like back in the County Championship. And that stress creates emotional issues.

You become grumpy. As much as you don't want to take your work home, you can't help it, because cricket captivates and engulfs you. Jess, my wife, has no interest in the game whatsoever, which is great, but sometimes I'll have to vent and she helps me understand and get to grips with certain things.

You start being short with your family. Things that usually you'd let lie, you don't let lie. You're worried about your last knock, you're worried about your next knock, you're worried about the series, you're worried about your position, you're worried about what's happening in the media. So it hampers your mood because it's impossible for it not to, and it hurts. It doesn't hurt your relationship, but it affects it, and it doesn't help the environment you're trying to create at home. Your wife's not going to stop loving you, but life isn't what it is when you're happy and you're on top of your game. It's just a horrible place to be.

My first experience of bad form was in South Africa in 2009/10. I remember very clearly that I was thinking about how I was going to get out instead of how I was going to score. I was coming back from Achilles surgery, my first proper injury – it had got infected, and what was meant to be one month off ended up being four.

Injuries are horrendous, a lot like bad form. You go to bed every night thinking, how's my injury? You wake up every morning thinking, how's my injury? You're worried about that first step you take out of bed, you're worried that you'll never play again, you're worried that you'll lose that happiness you're used to having every single day.

Rehabilitation is miserable. It's painful: all that time in the gym is painful, and so is being in the team one day and out of it the next. Feeling happy and relaxed in the dressing room, and walking into the dressing room when you're not fit, are chalk and cheese. You don't feel comfortable, you don't feel like you're a part of things, and someone's in your spot.

For a while, I wasn't sure I'd make that South Africa tour, and when I did I wasn't all there. Coming back into the team environment, I didn't know if my body was ready because I'd never gone through the rehab process before, and I hadn't played cricket competitively for a while. Then I had to start running around again; I was doing all the fielding drills thinking, this is going to be sore in the morning . . .

The whole thing was very, very draining. It fatigues you, and you can't get to the place that you should be in – just ask Chris Tremlett. In practice, I wasn't hitting the ball as well as I was used to, and in the first one-day international I missed a straight one from Albie Morkel, who clean-bowled me.

The first Test was a bit better: I scored 40 and 81 at Centurion to help save the game. But I also ran myself out at a crucial moment and played really, really badly for the rest of the series, averaging 11.20 in five innings.

Mentally, I was off the pace. I found it tough being back in South Africa. Because I'd got the numbers to back up the choice I'd made, things had changed and people sort of understood where I was coming from – there was a little more respect there. I was still under plenty of pressure, though, and along with the injury I wasn't as comfortable as

I needed to be to succeed. One way and another, I just didn't have the game.

Then we went to Bangladesh, where I made a couple of decent scores; the World T20 in the West Indies was great; and my son Dylan was born during it, which was amazing. But it would be silly to claim it had no impact on my game once I got back for the summer Tests.

I think any sportsman goes through a bit of a difficult phase when they've got a newborn baby, because sleep patterns and thought patterns are out of the window. In your personal life, it's the most incredible time, but at work you can't concentrate as well. Your mind isn't where it should be, even though it's exactly where it should be and that affects your technique.

Obviously you can't blame your family: you just enjoy them, and in the long term, it's brilliant to have something to engage with that isn't cricket. But, although people say, 'Oh, your kid doesn't care if you've had a bad day,' and they're right – you go home and your kid smiles at you whatever – you don't want to have too many bad days because it's you who's got to provide for that kid.

I did manage to get a few decent scores that summer, but didn't look convincing. By the time I was dropped for the limited-overs games I hadn't scored an international century in any format for forty-seven innings and nearly eighteen months.

What people often don't realise is that sportsmen are sensitive. A lot of us are sensitive souls, and a lot of us are *real* sensitive souls. Sport can have a macho culture – you play with aggression and sometimes you think you need to play up the bravado, when actually, deep down, you're thinking, I'm really worried about this. How should I be doing this?

Graeme Swann was an interesting one, because whenever he wasn't bowling well he'd just carry on in exactly the same jovial, piss-taking way. Maybe he could do that because he was secure in his spot in the team, but since he retired he's explained how that was just his method of dealing with stress. He used to try to talk his way out of it, and keep talking to keep himself sane. But if you weren't him you'd never have known that he was worried about anything.

That's the poker face I suppose you've got to wear, because there's a certain persona that gets you success on the sports field. But it's hard sometimes. We're not robots, we have emotions, and when we go through bad times at work we're like every single other person. It's just that what happens at our work is printed in the newspapers and our work is watched by millions of people on television. Our work is criticised, our work is tactically analysed, our work is technically analysed. We used to laugh about it in the dressing room – 'Whose turn is it this week?' – because the media will always be at somebody.

People like discussion points, and in this instance it would be whoever was struggling at the time. Yes, as players we're in a position that everyone thinks is the most amazing thing in the world, and it is. But when things are going badly, because it's hard to get away from it's even harder to handle.

If you're a lawyer going through a hard time and you've just lost a deal or a case, no one knows about it. Same in an accounting firm, a school, or whatever. Nobody knows what's going on in your life. When I'm struggling, though, I walk down the street and people say, 'Come on, buddy', and even though they're trying to be nice and give me confidence they don't. It's the same when my mum texts me, it's okay darling, I'm sure you'll go okay next time. It just makes me think, fuck, I'm worried.

What's weird is that bad form feels worse when the team's winning. Whatever's happening you feel like you're letting people down, but if the team's losing then so is everyone else and you're all feeling bad together. When the team's winning, though, when others are doing their jobs and you're not doing yours, you're the only one feeling bad, and that makes you feel worse. In the end, you're on your own.

In the time that I wasn't scoring we got a decent draw in South Africa, thrashed Bangladesh twice and won well against Pakistan. I started to wonder: are people watching me? Are people talking behind my back? How I am going here?

So I watched tapes of the 158 I made at Adelaide in December 2006, when I thought that I was batting at my best. I always compare myself to that. But it's difficult to see head movement and ball tracking on a screen, same as balance and weight – those things, you can only feel.

You can look at your set-up, though, and see that your trigger movements and your hands are always exactly the same – your technique is your technique. Sure, sometimes your movement might be a little bit late, or your bat might get a bit too far behind you, but that's still mental. It's so mental. I wasn't a different player, I just had a different psyche, and that meant I was looking for information, not watching the ball and thinking about how much fun batting is.

I decided I'd fly to Durban to work with Graham Ford. When I got there he started throwing at me, and after the third or fourth go he said, get your head into the ball. You're not getting your head into the ball. It's a fundamental basic that you've been doing your whole career, you're just not doing it.

Literally within minutes I was back playing at my best. My weight was perfectly positioned, and I thought, this feels so good, man. My head's going through the ball again, my weight's going through the ball when I drive it, it goes where I want it to go. When I defend it goes back to the bowler, and when I'm playing a pull shot it goes where I want to pull it.

During the previous year or so I'd been tentative. When I drove, the ball wasn't going and I was defending with the outside half or the inside half of my bat. But from that day onwards I was just going *bang-bang-bang*. I felt alive again, I went to Australia and boom: form.

Good form is everything bad form isn't. Good form is when you're totally at peace and at ease with what your game is, with where your game's at. Good form is keeping it simple, being clear in your approach and knowing what you want. Good form is not worrying about consequences. Good form is focusing on what you're going to deliver. Good form is not worrying about opposition, not worrying about how you're going to get out. Good form is knowing results will take care of themselves. Good form is taking things as they come. Good form is seeing ball and hitting ball. Good form is transferring practice into the game. Good form is people dropping catches. Good form is really enjoying your job. Good form is sleeping well at night. Good form is walking around with a smile on your face.

I've found it easier to find my form as I've got older. I deal with the media better, I understand my game better, I'm ready for good days and bad days. Will I score another run? Yes. Why will I score another run? Because I know I'm a very good player and I know that I'm able to deliver. I might be able to deliver this month or I might not be able to deliver this month, but I will deliver. And that's the way age takes you, that's what maturity does for you.

In my late twenties and early thirties I needed a couple of weeks of practice before I started playing well, but I'm much more comfortable in my game now. I had a four-month break before I played the 2014 Big Bash and it only took me three or four net sessions to be batting really well again, then in the 2015 CPL I hit 42 off twenty-six balls in my first innings. I've done it so many times, I know how simple I can make it in my head, and that gives me the confidence just to work on a select few drills, get my eyes right. Then

I'm good as gold, ready to go. The difference is quite amazing.

And sometimes, when you're in form, when the bat feels good in your hands and you're seeing the ball early, you reach the zone – that place everyone strives for, where you're just playing unbelievably well.

The first time I got there was probably when Brett Lee bounced me at the Oval in 2005, and it also happened during that 2006 innings in Adelaide. Oddly, that one hit me more or less from the start, which is very rare. Lee's second ball to me was clocked at 93 mph and I pulled it through midwicket easily.

I was just batting beautifully that day, and pretty early on I danced down the wicket and whacked Warnie for six over extra cover. We had a bit of a battle after that: he was obviously desperate to get me out, so lobbed up a few of his wide balls. I was waiting for him, really waiting; picking length, getting back on the crease and cutting him, not being tempted to slog into the leg side from outside my eyeline.

I've got to say, that Adelaide track is one of the best I've ever played on, and it was still pretty good when we came back in 2010. At the Gabba, in the first innings of the first Test, I'd made 43 out of 260, a total that left us well behind Australia. But we fought back so brilliantly that I didn't have to bat again – Strauss made a century, Trott made an unbeaten century, and Cook an unbeaten double century.

Australia then won the toss again, and within three overs,

Katich, Ponting and Clarke were gone. We got them all out for 245, a great effort on that pitch, and although we lost Strauss for 1, after that Cook and Trott batted for forty-seven overs, putting on 173.

It's pretty tough waiting so many hours to bat: you're concentrating hard and the adrenalin's going because it could be your time at any moment. I'd done the same in Brisbane and had got really bad pad-rash, so asked Colly if he wanted to go ahead of me for a while, then we could swap back, but he thought we were doing fine as we were. Then, about ten minutes later, we lost a wicket and I was thrust into it.

Early on, I ran down the wicket to Xavier Doherty, a left-arm spinner I'm certain they picked just to get at me, on the basis that there was no obvious right-arm option. I was planning to smash him out of the ground but miscued and the ball landed just over cover's head, but after that I played a flawless innings.

My celebration when I got from 99 to 100 was pretty special, because of how painful the previous few months had been. Then, twelve runs later, Peter Siddle decided to put three men on the boundary and start bouncing me. So I stood like a baseball player telling myself, I'm not going to fall over and die here. I'm not just going to let you dictate terms and bowl bouncers at me while I duck and weave. You want to bowl bouncers at me, I'm going to try to crack you for six every single ball. There's only going to be one winner here, and I'm not backing down.

So I smashed him for a couple of fours, a confrontation that got me in the zone, and I kept on going. I got stuck on 158 for a bit, making sure I wasn't getting out for that again, but my second hundred still only took 125 balls. I properly screamed when I brought it up, because it's a very, very special feeling to get to 200, especially against Australia, in Australia.

Eventually, Doherty had me caught at slip for 227, and fifty runs later we declared on 620 with a lead of 375. We then got them three down for 134, but Clarke and Mike Hussey, both excellent players of spin, batted very well. Swanny bowled thirty-four overs in a row, from the morning session all the way through the afternoon and most of the evening, but they defeated him from over and around the wicket.

So, even though I'm a no-hope bowler, Straussy chucked me the ball just before the end of the day to see if I could make something happen, and in my second over one bounced and turned a bit more than Clarke expected. He should probably have rocked back and whacked it, but because he was trying to be careful edged onto his thigh pad and was caught at short leg. I guess I had a bit of a golden arm that day.

The next morning, it only took us twenty overs to pick up the final six wickets and win by an innings, doing the same at Melbourne and Sydney to give the Aussies a proper hiding. They were a team in transition, whereas we had some fantastic players, and all of them were performing brilliantly.

Then, the following summer, we beat Sri Lanka. I didn't get many in the first two Tests, but in the third, at Southampton, I made 72 and 85. India arrived after that, and though we'd always have been favourites in English conditions they'd won on their last visit and still had legends like Tendulkar, Dhoni and Dravid.

They won the first toss and bowled, which you might do at Lord's, as the wicket tends to flatten out. This one was incredibly green – the kind we wanted to play on to make the most of our home advantage. I wasn't that surprised to find myself going in at 26–2, and at the start I really struggled; the ball was swinging and seaming, and scoring was difficult.

Then they started bowling at me from wide of the crease and to wide of off stump, obviously a ploy they'd thought would frustrate me, but I was actually quite comfortable with it. The ball was still new and the track was fresh, so if they'd have stayed straight to make me play, and Ishant Sharma had angled it into me, I'd have found it harder. There was movement in the air, off the pitch and with the Duke, so I might have missed one and been bowled or lbw, I might have nicked one and I might have gone on a bad run.

Instead, they tried to break my concentration and get me chasing something wide, hoping I'd nick to slip or the keeper. And so I said to myself, listen, the wicket's doing plenty, but if they're bowling out there they can't get you out. When they start bowling straight, that's when you've got issues. Stay disciplined and don't touch the ball outside off stump – just leave it, let them bowl there.

I showed as much restraint as I could, and eventually they changed their line. That forced me to start playing more, so I stood outside my crease to negate the seam, and I was still there when play finished early because of rain and bad light. I'd made 22 off seventy-three balls, and it had been tough.

At the start of day two, still standing down the track, I eventually got to my slowest Test hundred, off 216 balls. But as the wicket started to do less I capitalised and smashed it everywhere. My second hundred came in 110 balls.

About halfway through it I found myself in a different place. I slogged Praveen Kumar over his head and whacked Ishant, then took Suresh Raina for four, six, two and four to bring up my fourth fifty, which came from twenty-five balls. Yep, I was in the zone.

In the zone, everything is simple. I'm so focused on dealing what I need to deal with that I don't even know I'm there. There are no worries. I'm just looking to score, to hit the ball, to be attacking, to dominate, to be aggressive. I'm hitting balls where I want to hit balls. Against spinners, I'm using my feet; against seamers, I'm walking across my stumps. I'm looking to play with power and in power areas, down the ground, through cover, through midwicket and square leg. I'm not looking for finesse, I'm looking for strong shots. I'm looking to leave positively. I'm looking to run well between wickets. I might talk to my partner in between balls and overs, but I'm just so chilled and caught up in what I'm doing that I don't really notice much. I'm just so unaware of what's going on around me, and so zeroed in on what's about to be delivered, that nothing else matters. I'm totally focused and engrossed in making sure I get what I want, so consequences and negativity don't come anywhere near my thinking.

It's funny, the phrase people use to talk about that scenario is 'seeing it big', but what's actually happening is you're seeing it slow. You have so long to watch the ball, find the ball and hit the ball, even though the time period as a whole, the length of your innings, passes really fast. Everything just happens so well and so perfectly that the world is your oyster. Nothing bad can happen to you at that point in time. Nothing.

Though you usually get into the zone in the middle of an innings – it never starts at the beginning and lasts all the way through – you only come out of it once it's over. And if it's gone on for a while, it takes a long time to actually understand what's happened and for what you've accomplished to sink in. Two and a half months before writing this, I scored 355 not out and I still don't feel like I've fully absorbed it.

Ricky Ponting wrote that the zone was something he only experienced a few times in his career. But he had the ability to play cover drives and pull shots whenever he wanted and never really look in any sort of trouble because that was just his greatness; he could take attacks apart with ease, whereas I found it a little bit more difficult. I had to make a really concerted effort to make things happen, and maybe that's why getting in the zone happened for me more often. I needed it more than he did.

It was a great feeling to find it against India at Lord's in 2011 and set up a series; my 202 not out helped us to a big first innings total, 474–8 declared. We then bowled them out for 286, but after that Ishant knocked over our middle order. He's a very good bowler, just inconsistent, and that morning he got rid of three of us very quickly. Within two days I went from 202 to 1, hero to zero, and that's Test cricket. One minute you're walking out to the loudest applause ever, the next you're trudging back in and the whole of Lord's is just this deathly silence.

I also got into the zone for a little while at Headingley, when Morné Morkel came around the wicket to bounce me with a leg-side field. And I was still there a bit later when Steyn took the second new ball and I was hitting him over his head and pulling him through midwicket without really knowing what I was doing, but like it was the easiest thing in the world.

When I think about others I've seen in the zone, the innings that always comes to me first is Adam Gilchrist at Perth in 2006. At the time, the hundred he scored was the second-fastest in Test history, off fifty-seven balls, though it's now the third, after Misbah-ul-Haq equalled Viv Richards's record of fifty-six. In particular, the way he went after Monty Panesar, who'd got him out earlier in the match, was incredible. Though he had the advantage of hitting with the Fremantle Doctor – no way could Monty bowl to him from the end that he was on at – he was so at one with himself, it was frightening.

I was at long-on, and while it was great to watch because it was Adam Gilchrist in full swing, I was playing against him and that was demoralising. It just took the heart out of us; if our tour wasn't bad enough already, that finished it off right there. Mentally, it was the most fatiguing hour and a half of cricket, seeing this guy destroy our attack and guarantee we'd lose the Ashes we'd worked so hard to win. The Aussies already had their hands on our throat, and he broke our neck.

Another knock that springs to mind is when Sehwag made 83 off sixty-eight balls at Chennai in 2008 – no matter where we bowled, he kept whacking it. And the way Mahendra Singh Dhoni finishes off innings in limited-overs cricket – in the 2011 World Cup final he sent himself up the order and made 91 not out – makes it seem like he finds the zone a lot. He's just got crazy, crazy calmness, and incredible hand–eye coordination, which is how he can manipulate the ball so skilfully and powerfully.

Shane Watson at Melbourne in 2011 is another one-day innings that stands out. We made 294, not bad at the time, and he smacked 161 not out off 150 balls. To hit like that and bat through the innings – that was the real thing.

There are loads of other batters I've seen perform really well, like Kallis and Trott, or Cook in the 2010/11 Ashes.

But to me, that was form. The zone is different; it's when you're delivering knockout blows.

The best batting I've seen from an England player was Ian Bell in the 2013 Ashes. That wasn't fill-your-boots time against a poor attack, and he didn't grind them out either. He was dominant in the series, and the difference between the teams.

Bell was so brilliant in the way that he cover-drove the ball, the way he pulled, the way he cut, the way he glanced – he just destroyed Australia, he was a complete freakshow. He was totally at ease, and had so much time to see the ball, pick length and play.

He scored a century at Trent Bridge – the only one on either side – then at Lord's came in at 28–3 to make another. His 60 at Old Trafford helped us save the match and retain the urn, and then a magnificent 113 at Chester-le-Street was crucial in winning the Test and clinching the series. He got a lot of adulation in the dressing room.

In Durham, though, he was helped by Stuart Broad, a very good bowler who's suffered from a volume of cricket; it's impossible for him to be at his fastest all the time. So, unfortunately, he's had to hold back and produce spells when they count, and that's what he's done throughout his career – though this last year or so, he's gone up a level.

It must have been frustrating for him. But then, when you're out of the side and you step back, you remember that these fast bowlers are rare creatures; what they put their bodies through is a very special practice.

Broad's an argumentative, stubborn guy, who says and does impulsive things that sometimes make no sense.

The upside of that is he's got such belief in himself and wants what he wants so much that he'll do anything to achieve it. It's those kinds of guys – guys who don't sit on the fence, but make decisions and stand by them – who find themselves in the zone most often, and conjure those moments of brilliance.

In the final Test of the 2009 Ashes Broad produced a devastating spell out of nowhere, taking five wickets in eleven overs to rip through Australia and settle the series. Against India at Trent Bridge in 2012 he took five wickets in four overs, including a hat-trick. Against New Zealand at Lord's in 2013, seven wickets in eleven overs. Against Australia at Chester-le-Street in 2013, six wickets in 7.3 overs. Against Australia at Trent Bridge in 2015, 8–15 in 9.3 overs.

It's not just a confidence issue – it's also partly rhythm. Even when you're just running for fun, sometimes you find that groove and go easier and faster than when you don't. And fast bowling's a rhythm activity: you're sprinting in and you need your legs to be light, you need to hit that crease, get through your action and get the ball to go where you want it.

But there's something more to it than that. That spell at Durham, for example, at the end of a hard Test and towards the end of a hard series: that was Broad understanding what a situation needed and forcing himself on it. His confrontational, spontaneous personality urged him to dig up the aggression, which increased his pace by 5 mph. That helped him get the ball reversing, and within an hour he'd won us a Test it looked like we were losing. Certain players just know when the time is right and can take themselves to another place, and that's why he has more fourth-innings wickets in England wins than anyone else, and some amazing memories.

Being in the zone is the best feeling in cricket, one of the best feelings in the world. It's not as great as the birth of your child, but you savour it in a different way because you don't know when it's coming. And you definitely don't know when it's coming back.

On Paradise

On Pressure

A ndy Flower once asked me why I didn't get cross when I got out. What do you mean, do I not get cross when I get out? I replied.

You just don't look like you get cross, he said.

What, so I should walk into the dressing room and start hitting things and ranting and raving, because that shows you that I'm cross? How do you know what I'm feeling inside? How do you know what anyone's feeling inside?

The truth is, with the way that I played and with the weight of expectation that I have every single time I walk out onto a cricket field, it should be me who's shouting and screaming the loudest when I get out. That's exactly what should be happening, because I'm the one who's under the most pressure.

But that's not how I ever saw it. I walked in and thought, no, I'm not going to do it because it's not fair on the other guys in there. It just makes the dressing room uncomfortable, so why would I do that? I'm not going to do that.

I know it's a cliché, but for me, pressure is a privilege. The feeling of dealing successfully with pressure is far greater than the feeling of dealing with something that's easy. And I never forget and never take for granted the fact that I do something that so many people would love to do.

I always felt that I could get really good at dealing with pressure, because I've always enjoyed the challenge of practising hard and then taking the self-belief that gives you out into the middle. I've always told myself that no situation is too hard to deal with, and if you want to be valued as an important and integral part of a team, if you want to be proud of yourself as a player and a person, you've got to be able to deal with difficult situations.

Life is about learning, and life is about dealing with unexpected challenges; the pressure you find on a cricket field sets you up for anything that can happen off it. In business I've made stupid decisions that have, on occasion, lost me a lot of money. Annoying, but the best way of dealing with it is to stay calm, then work out why I made a particular decision. I've done that so many times in my playing career I've created a method that works for me, focusing on taking positives and understanding negatives.

When you understand negatives, you understand pressure. And when you appreciate that there are two different parts of your brain, the emotional and the logical, you have a much better idea of how you work.

Over the last five or six years I've done a lot of work with Mark Borden, a sports psychologist and a really good guy, who's taught me that I'm much more of a logical person than an emotional one. In 2014, for example, I played a T20 game for Surrey at Gloucester. We were in the field, Ian Cockbain hit a ball way up into the air in my direction and I immediately thought, I'm going to have to get this. It was a hard catch, a real running-in-hard catch, but while I was on my way I started saying to myself, you've caught so many of these balls before, this is as easy as practice. You've done a thousand of these before – just take it. Get to the ball, hands up, get it done.

As soon as I did, the guys ran up to me and said, you made that catch look so simple. And that for me was an immediate win: I'd managed to use logic to control emotion, under pressure.

When there isn't time to go through that mental process you force it by volume of practice. I couldn't just go and stand at slip tomorrow and say, okay, I'm happy, because I know I haven't caught a ball there; instead I'd be worrying about how the hell was I going to do it. Whereas at gully, I'd feel completely different: I was a gully fielder and practised the position every single day. Duncan Fletcher and Andy Flower were just outstanding in the way they hit balls at you, bottom right, top left, bottom left, bottom right, and that made you confident. I didn't drop too many there because I knew that I'd trained and trained and trained, so logic told me there was no need to feel emotional pressure.

At the time of writing, I'm not playing Test cricket and so the pressure I'm under is different. I go for a lot of money in the franchise-tournament auctions, which means there's a responsibility to perform, as well as to help younger players and guide the team. It's different from a Test match, though, and I really miss the fierce competition of the longer game. I miss it a lot.

On the other hand, there's also pressure that you can do without. After Michael Vaughan retired I asked his wife Nichola if all the commentary that he was doing, plus his newspaper column, meant that he was away from home even more than when he was playing. And she said, KP, the difference now is when he's at home, he's at home.

That's a very, very interesting point, and it's how I am at the moment. When I'm at home, I'm at home. I don't worry about my job. I've got set contracts around the world and I go out and perform, but that's it. Whereas when you're on England duty you're at work all the time

The media does an amazing job publicising the game, but the way they apply pressure in the UK has an effect.

They have the power to shape the public's perception of a player because the pen is mightier than the bat. They create the public figure you become, your public persona, and that persona may not go down too well with the public. People often say I'm nothing like the guy they read or hear about, but that's the way of the world.

Sometimes all you can do is get out of the way. Brett Lee's bowling at the Oval in 2005
was some of the quickest I've ever faced

I never felt completely in control against Murali, as he was so difficult to pick until the ball had left his hand – playing him was like facing a quick

Not only could Swanny clean people up in the second innings, he also had the ability to knock them over during the first

In the theatre of Warne. Facing the jovial assassin at the MCG in 2006

With Rahul Dravid, one of the best players of spin I've ever known, during the 2010 IPL tournament

Checking Duckworth–Lewis
with Michael Vaughan
against South Africa in 2005

With captain Cook on day three of the Adelaide Test in 2010 – his phenomenal mental
strength made him great to bat with

Captaining England against India in 2008, and celebrating Swann (with his back to the camera) taking his second Test wicket in his first Test over

Strauss leading the team out at Lord's against South Africa in 2012. I always felt the captaincy enabled him to come out of his shell as a player

Dream Team

Virender Sehwag

Sachin Tendulkar

Ricky Ponting

Jacques Kallis

Kumar Sangakkara

Andrew Flintoff

Dream Team

Adam Gilchrist (wk)

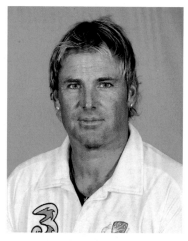

Shane Warne (c)

Jimmy Anderson

Shoaib Akhtar

Glenn McGrath

Muttiah Muralitharan

For similar reasons, questions in press conferences are often not about the game, but about some side issue, personal if possible, that they think's controversial and will get the most hits on their website and sell the most papers. They need to do that more than they need to be interesting, original or honest, and that's why you find my name in the headlines of stories that have nothing to do with me.

In the subcontinent, it's a bit different. Cricket's a religion, so Indian cricketers are treated like gods, and with that comes a lot of responsibility, a lot of expectation. For that reason, their great players are the level-headed ones, the ones who can put the hype to one side and keep things simple, because the media can control their career; the only way to survive is to ignore it.

Initially, when I was picked for England I didn't worry about it. I was only twenty-five, I was confident, and I was focused.

That's why, in the early summer of 2005, when England played their Test series against Bangladesh, I thought nothing of badgering Michael Vaughan. I was texting him all the time, saying I'm ready, I'm ready, I'm ready, I'm ready. Give me a game, I want to play against Australia.

He replied, saying chill, you'll get your turn, but I couldn't let it go. I'd had so much success in one-day cricket that I was convinced I could do it in the longer format too, I was batting well and I was desperate to play in the Ashes.

So when I got picked, for the first Test, I was more

excited than anything else. We knew we were underdogs, but we were sure we could compete.

The day before we played at Lord's, I told the media: 'Whatever happens, the sun will rise the next morning. If I get a duck, who cares? I am going to enjoy my Test debut and not be a nervous wreck.' I meant it.

I slept well that night, and then, in the morning, the atmosphere in the ground was as great as any I've experienced in my career. Walking through the Long Room when we came out to field, the noise was incredible, unbelievable, deafening. It made everybody feel like they were ten feet tall, like we could take on the Australians and dominate them. And we produced a couple of great sessions with the ball, running through them for 190 in 40.2 overs.

The problem came when we batted. I went in at 18–3, and was still on 0 when Belly went, then on 2 when Freddie went. Suddenly we were 21–5 and Glenn McGrath had taken all the wickets.

Geraint Jones and I built a partnership of 58, both of us whacking boundaries, but Brett Lee got him for 30, and then Ashley Giles for 11 with the last ball of the day. I was 29 not out, but England were 90–7.

That night, I had dinner with my parents and brother, and by a quarter to eight I was done. I remember saying, sorry, I am mentally so shot I'm going to have to go to bed. I never knew that Test cricket was that hard; I guess that's what you'd call pressure.

Even though I'd done okay, there were mixed emotions. Runs only mean something if you're winning the game. If the team's in a bad position you can't swan around and be happy about life because, at the end of the day, you're suffering with everyone else. You've got to find ways to help the situation, which for me was to get runs. So because I was riding the crest of a wave with my batting and not really thinking about too much, I did what I always did and just went for it.

I guess I was lucky that the way Glenn McGrath bowled – hitting a length – complemented the way I batted – searching for the ball, getting my head to it and going at it. I didn't go looking to hit sixes – all that happened was the ball turned up in my areas so I went *smack, bang*. Maybe the circumstances helped too, because I knew that there was only the tail left, but basically I was just enjoying facing those guys and being successful against them, showing people that my technique was fine for Test cricket. That innings proved that I could play.

In the end, though, it wasn't enough. I made 57, but we finished 35 behind on first innings, and though I got 64 not out in our second, we ended up getting absolutely slaughtered, losing by 239 runs.

I know Vaughany's said since that all our batters froze apart from me, but it's hard for me to say because I wasn't really thinking about it. It's totally different, being a captain and being a player on debut. On debut, you just mind your business, try to score your runs, and try to make an impression on the game and the team. You don't worry about how Joe Soap's doing or what's being said in the dressing room; you're not interested in that at all.

Looking back at how the other guys got out in the first innings, either caught at slip or bowled, it does seem like maybe the fear of McGrath got to them. It stands to reason, I guess. The team were on a roll, so the expectation was huge – the whole country was expecting us to perform. And even though a fair few of the guys hadn't played Australia before, they'd all grown up with them punishing England, whereas I wasn't scarred by that at all. I was a lot more positive and a lot more aggressive than them, and that meant my technique on the day was excellent.

It's hard to describe exactly how I felt, but I was running high on adrenalin, I didn't feel threatened by the bowling, and that gave me the confidence to attack it. I knew that I just needed to go out there and club the ball, and club the ball I did.

Obviously the press panicked because of how badly we lost, but Fletcher and Vaughan kept everything and everyone very calm. Before the second Test we did absolutely nothing, just chilled, and then trained really well in the couple of days leading up to it.

Then when we got to Birmingham Vaughan sat us down and reiterated how he wanted us to play. Right guys, he said, we fight fire with fire. We want to smash this ball.

I think that was the moment we all committed to the approach. We knew we needed to up our game or else we were going to get clobbered again, so agreed that we'd play the same aggressive way we had in the one-dayers.

I didn't actually see McGrath get injured on that first morning at Edgbaston, but they showed him limping off the field on the big screen about half an hour after it happened. Then, when we got off the field after the warm-up, people were saying that he was out of the game, and that was a huge, huge thing. Much as you enjoy testing yourself against the best players, you're pleased when they're out; knowing we didn't have to deal with such a superstar, that was advantage England. No McGrath gave us all the encouragement we needed to go out there and punish the bowling, much more so than them winning the toss and putting us in – which, though the media loved it, we hardly mentioned.

And we really did punish the bowling. In particular, Tres batted brilliantly – to get 90 off 102 balls on the first day of a Test is seriously special. He is, without doubt, the best batsman I played with for England: obviously he scored runs and he scored hundreds, but just as important was the way that he scored them. He was positive, he hit sixes, he played beautiful cover drives, he picked up off his legs and he played the pull shot; he was just superb all round, and made it look so easy. He didn't really move his feet much, but he was technically very sound, getting into good positions with his trigger, getting his head into good positions, then he used wonderful eyes and hands to smack the ball. Compared to me, he was a bit more orthodox, and because he was left-handed played more on the off side. It's just a pity that his career was cut short, because with his ball-striking and sheer talent he would have had phenomenal numbers and become a great of the game.

Because we were batting so well, the Aussies were forced to bring Warne on for the fourteenth over, only for us to go after him as well – Strauss took three quick fours and Tres whacked the third ball he faced for six. It gave all the players confidence, watching their big talisman get knocked around a bit, especially with McGrath gone.

I came in that day at 170–3, and though Vaughan went quickly, after that, Freddie and I built a big partnership. We were super-aggressive and super-positive – not thinking about getting out at all. I was just saying, if Warnie gives it air, hit him into the stands. If Brett Lee pitches short we'll hit him into the stands too. If it's your area, smash it out of the ground. And Freddie had this saying, 'If it's up, it's off': basically, anything flighted, he went after with his big power.

We put on 101 in sixteen overs: Freddie got 68 with six fours and five sixes, and I got 71 with ten fours and one six. Then our last two wickets added 59, and we were set – 407 runs in 79.2 overs was pretty incredible, even though we were all out by the end of the day.

On day two, we bowled pretty well to knock Australia over for 308, so even when we collapsed in the second innings there was no feeling in the dressing room of *here we go again* ... We were still in a very good position in the game and confident we could finish it off.

And we backed it up in the field. At the end of the third day Australia were eight down and still 107 runs short of their target, so we felt very confident about what was coming next. We'd talked about what we were going to do, we'd done it and it had worked.

On the morning of the final session we were ready to win. The atmosphere around the ground was electric: it seemed like everyone had already started drinking, four or five pints in already.

And the Barmy Army were very, very loud and boisterous, singing all the songs. They probably thought it could all be over in twenty minutes, so really went for it.

But, just as he had the previous evening, Shane Warne went about his business in a very Shane Warne way – he and Brett Lee batted beautifully, they really did. The wicket was flat so we couldn't aggressively bounce them, and they took the attack to us, which made for a very, very interesting day. It started off carefree and relaxed, us thinking that we were going to get a quick win, and then became super-intense.

We were starting to get worried, but Warnie hitting his wicket with 62 runs still required got our hopes up again. But then Lee and Kasprowicz batted as well as they have ever batted, the runs started ticking down and it got nerve-racking again. None of us had been expecting it to go like that.

The Australians in the crowd were clapping every run, counting them down by singing a version of 'Ten Green Bottles'. I was fielding in the covers, I was fielding at long off – I was a boundary rider, so was all over the place. I'm fidgety at the best of times, but when I'm nervous I'm very fidgety, and that day I was ridiculously fidgety, biting my nails like mad. I remember Michael Vaughan had to move me back to my spot on numerous occasions, so I marked the grass to show myself where to stand, only to keep veering away from it again.

I was feeling sick. It had taken so much out of us, but we'd got Australia on the ropes by playing such a good Test match, and now we were going to fall at the final hurdle. Twenty runs to win. Vaughany brought Freddie back and he hit Lee on the fingers, so there was a break in play that increased the tension. Then, with 15 required, Kasprowicz sliced over the slips and it headed down to Simon Jones at third man. We'd been waiting for our chance and there it was – he ran in, dived ... but couldn't quite get there.

As they got to within single figures of the target, Vaughany had almost all of us on the boundary, to make them face as many balls as possible. With only four needed, Steve Harmison bowled a full toss to Lee, who smashed it out to Jones, sweeping on the off side. I remember watching the ball going and going, thinking, that's it – we've lost. We're two–nil down. But Jones stopped it, threw it back in and then the delivery after next we got Lee's wicket. It was an absolutely amazing rush of euphoria and relief.

We had a very, very long day and night celebrating after that, a pub crawl down Broad Street, just all of us absolutely ecstatic. It was an incredible release.

At Old Trafford we again played well, but I didn't score many. Lee got me in the first innings, and in the second McGrath came around the wicket first up. I guess he thought, we haven't tried this, he's knocked us around quite a bit in the first two Test matches, he's obviously got a weakness somewhere, let's see.

I was pretty shocked. I wasn't expecting that at all, and when I saw he was doing it, I assumed he'd take an aggressive line, that he'd bowl short and attack me. I definitely wasn't ready for a yorker. I didn't pick it up, and *bang*: gone for a golden duck! At the time, I wasn't sure how it'd happened, but afterwards I realised that he just completely out-thought me and I was on my bike.

But it didn't matter, because Michael Vaughan set up the game for us, playing beautifully and with sheer class for his big hundred. Decent contributions from Belly, Freddie and Geraint Jones left us with 444, a pretty good total, especially when we then bowled them out for 302. Gilo did for both of the openers, but the star was Simon Jones, who had Ponting caught at gully and then took Australia's last five wickets.

Some fast hitting meant that we could declare just before stumps on day four, setting Australia 422 to win. Even though we didn't have any success that evening, the next morning we thought we had a good chance – the wicket was up and down and we were bowling well. Freddie was charging in, Harmy and Hoggard were in the game and Simon got Michael Clarke with an incredibly good reversing inswinger that he left.

Batting looked ridiculously hard from the start to the close – for everyone but Ricky Ponting. Under extraordinary pressure, he played as though it was a day-one wicket against a club side and delivered an absolutely unbelievable innings, the best I've seen. Graeme Smith's 154 not out at Edgbaston in 2008 compares as a captain's knock, but this was better. The attack was better, the shots were better, the pitch was worse and the stakes were much, much higher. He was out there for nearly seven hours, more than two hours longer than anyone else managed that Test and in the worst conditions, knowing all along that failure meant defeat. Just huge.

Obviously we wanted to win, especially as we got so close, but weren't disappointed – we didn't even have time to think about being disappointed As soon as the game was over, Michael Vaughan pulled us into a huddle and, right there and then, he told us: this is a victory. Have a look at the Australians, celebrating a draw. How often have you ever seen them celebrating a draw like that? We've got them, if they're celebrating a draw. All those great players are on that balcony, screaming, hugging, kissing each other almost. If that's what they're doing for a draw in this series, we can beat Australia. We believed him.

The build-up to Trent Bridge was again low-key, and again the crowd were absolutely fantastic. One of the things people remember is Gary Pratt, our sub fielder, running out Ricky Ponting with a direct hit, and Ponting losing his rag. I didn't actually see it, but we were all pretty amused. Punter was constantly looking for excuses that whole series, and we could see that the little things were starting to affect the Aussies. Again, we dominated the Test, making them follow on for the first time in seventeen years, and they set us 129 to win.

We started okay – Tres scored 27 in five overs – but Warnie got him with his first ball, then Vaughan for a duck, so when Strauss goes I'm in at 57–3. I've got the driest mouth, because for the first time in my career, I'm nervous. I'm playing to put England one up with one to play in the Ashes, which Australia have held for sixteen years. But what's really getting to me is how small the total is. To lose from here would be a killer, and the enormity of everything that's happening – the pressure of the battle in front of me right here and now – has completely got to me.

Warne decides to come around the wicket to me, a very defensive ploy. He's thinking that if he bowls from over, I'll be able to whack us to our target just by getting a few slog-sweeps away. He still bowls me a full toss to smash into the stand, except I find myself padding it up instead because I'm scared of getting out, and then I miss out on a few other boundary balls for the same reason. I'm looking for the negatives, thinking about what could go wrong. We've all worked so hard to get here, playing such good cricket, that we really can't mess it up on the last day, and I feel like it's all on me to win the game for everyone.

I scramble to 23, but I can only get boundaries off Shaun Tait – a top edge, and two gifts on my pads. Then Lee bowls me a full one, I see it beautifully and go to punch it through the covers. Next thing I know, I've been caught behind. I've no idea how the hell I nicked that ball; I must have been hesitant without realising. I froze.

We need 26 to win with five wickets left, but Freddie goes two overs later and Geraint Jones in the one after that. We're in trouble. But somehow, Gilo and Hoggard get us over the line, and we only need a draw at the Oval to win the series.

It was an incredible time. We were actually quite surprised by it all, by how well we were doing, because we were playing that great Australian side with all those great players, and by how mad the country went. It really taught me to appreciate how wonderful our support is, and how privileged we are to play in front of such amazing crowds.

If you have a look around the world, you don't see many Test grounds that are sold out, but in England it's almost guaranteed every single time you play. That summer was something else, though. The weather was good, the wickets were outstanding, the games were on terrestrial TV and everyone was into them. We just couldn't believe how the grounds were filling up, even on the final days, how many people were queuing to come in and how many couldn't get in. I don't think that's ever happened before.

I'm sure that part of it was down to it being an Ashes series. Test cricket is the greatest battle in sport, and England versus Australia the greatest battle in Test cricket. That's why the games are watched by everybody around the world. There's nothing like it.

There was quite a long break before the Oval. Again, we kept things relaxed.

Even though I hadn't scored many runs since the first innings at Edgbaston, I had no worries at all. I was young, I was living the dream and I was batting well. I was seeing the ball and hitting the ball, so had no problem forgetting what happened at Trent Bridge. I had no experience of bad things happening, so I didn't think about them happening. I was just loving every single day.

So that's how much pressure I put on myself: none. But I did feel pressure from the media. In those days I was still reading the papers, and with me having won a whole four caps, obviously they were wondering whether I was good enough, so were dissecting my method. Everybody had had something to say about it – everybody, including some very well-known and very well-respected figures. I remember Geoffrey Boycott saying at the time that he thought I was too leg-side dominant and got too far across my stumps – basically that I was just a one-day player with no future in Test cricket.

People were also questioning my mentality as well as my technique – I'd got a 50, a 60 and a 70, but hadn't got myself a hundred. I knew that was pretty harsh, seeing as I'd scored 301 runs in the series, but I couldn't help thinking about it, which gave me a bit of a tricky week.

I got over it, though, because I was strong enough to back myself. I knew how comfortable I felt at the crease, so knew it was just a matter of time before I got to three figures.

On the first morning at the Oval, we were pleased to win the toss, and Strauss made a beautiful hundred. I got out softly, trying to flick Warne through midwicket, but that was the kind of shot I played, so I told myself it was important to carry on in the same way.

The 373 that we ended up with was only a goodish score. A competitive score, but not the kind of score that was totally out of range. The Australians were still walking around with a big reputation, and we hadn't got enough to guarantee a draw, so we were disappointed. We expected better of ourselves, and I expected better of myself.

All the more so when Justin Langer and Matthew Hayden came out and both got tons, their first of the series. But then, after we lost a fair bit of play to rain, we were pretty surprised when Langer and Damien Martyn took the light at the end of day three with their team still 97 runs behind. You understand it from a batter's perspective – you don't want to get out – but we thought they'd try to nail it down and be ultra-aggressive. We thought that this great Australian side, needing to win the Test, would have said, we're coming for you here. But they chose the negative option.

The following morning, Freddie bowled one of the greatest spells I've ever seen. Eleven and half overs straight, all the way through a session, taking 3 for 24. Insane.

Vaughan kept telling him to come off, and he was saying,

no, I'm bowling, I'm bowling. And yes, I know it was a great over that he sent down to Langer and Ponting at Edgbaston, but that was only seven balls. Here he used adrenalin, he used skill, he used fitness, he used mental strength; he used everything to get through that final spell. It was the fifth Test, he'd played the other four, and we all knew how injury-prone Freddie was. But on that day he delivered, and to run in in the way that he did to set the match up for us was amazing. He forced the game to go as he wanted it to. It's not very often you see Australians fear an opponent, but they feared Freddie. They couldn't handle his pressure.

At the start of the final day we were 34–1, 40 runs ahead. A long way from home. I was having breakfast in our hotel, and saw on the back page of a newspaper that England needed a hero. I am going to be that hero, I tell myself. I am going to be that hero.

Tres and Vaughany get us going really well; Vaughany's batting beautifully again. But then, with the score on 67, he edges McGrath behind and Gilchrist takes a great catch. I'm in the viewing area, watching through the window, so wish Belly luck on his way out and go to pad up. There's kit everywhere and a couple of bowlers asleep – they don't tend to watch much.

Then, as I'm strapping on my back pad, there's a great roar. I look up at the TV to see that Belly's gone first ball. Suddenly I'm panicking – I've got to get out there right away. I'm flapping through my five sets of gloves, looking for the ones I've marked '1', and can't find them, but at least I don't have to deal with all that time watching, waiting and worrying. I'm chucked right into the cauldron. I find my gloves, put my helmet on and go out.

Walking down the pavilion steps I look around; the ground is absolutely rammed. Again, the support is phenomenal. I feel the pressure, but I'm excited by the opportunity to get our team home – that's why I'm here. I say 'bad luck' to Belly, not that he's listening, and make my way to the middle.

I don't know the exact state of the game – how many runs we're ahead or how many overs are left – but it doesn't really matter. We need to bat time, we need to make sure we don't get bowled out cheaply, and, if possible, we need to score at a rate that means the Aussies can't overtake us. Time's with us, but it's against us if we play badly. I just need to bat. But if I don't, we're going to have a problem.

I feel great as I take guard, my hands perfect on the handle. I look around the field and settle into my stance, and in comes McGrath. It's not really registered that this is his hat-trick ball, but I'm expecting him to attack my stumps – only he bounces me! I'm absolutely suckered by the double bluff, take a hit on the shoulder and the fielders go crazy appealing for a catch. I panic for a second, but Billy Bowden's shaking his head and that calms my nerves.

Next over, Warne beats me with a big turner, and this time I do edge it. Gilly can't hold it, so pokes it across to Hayden. Who drops it!

Then I pull McGrath for four. Lee comes on and I take four off his first ball with a drive down the ground. Two dots, then Lee fires a full one outside my off stump. I go again, nick it again and turn again. It's going straight to Warnie at first slip – he's that far back because Lee's bowling so fast – and I watch it track right into his hands. He's got a hell of a safe pair, so I think that's it: I'm out. He drops it! My stomach's all over the place, the relief is amazing, but I don't smile. We've just lost two wickets, which is not a smiling matter, and we're so desperate to win the series.

I watch the replay and think the same as when Lee got me at Trent Bridge: how the hell can I nick a ball that's so full? I just can't understand how I could nick a ball like that. But I need to get straight, so tell myself, right, I've got to get my game on here. I've got to play well.

There's not long to go until lunch and we're not in terrible shape. I slog-sweep Warnie for two sixes in the same over. He's not pleased. But, like the champion he is, he quickly fights back. He gets Tres lbw, and then four overs later has Freddie caught and bowled. We're 126–5, 133 ahead and down to our last pair of batters, with plenty of time left to play. We're in real strife.

I watch Lee get ready for the last over before lunch, then he races in at ridiculous pace – the first ball's back of a length and cracks me in the ribs. You sometimes hear people say, if you get hurt, don't rub it, but if it hurts, I'm rubbing it. Why wouldn't I? What's Lee going to do? Aim for the same spot again? I've made a mistake, but it's not like I'm a tail-ender who can't defend myself. I'm not interested in the bravado of cricket. If it's sore, rub it.

Kirk Russell, our physio, comes on and gives me some freeze spray – I switch off for that, then snap myself back in when it's time to start again. I'm watching the ball, but I know that at 95 mph, which is how fast it's coming at me, I'm just playing on instinct. And obviously I get a proper short one, this is some serious speed, fearsome, ferocious, and even though I'm getting a view of Lee's action it doesn't matter. I wear that one under the armpit. And then another one knocks me off my feet as I glove it – probably the quickest bouncer I've ever faced. It's enough to get me down the other end, and Colly plays out the final three deliveries.

It wasn't much fun, but I know a brilliant over when I don't see one. It properly roughed me up, and on my way off, I'm thinking how it's brilliant of Australia to have attacked me like that, because if they'd got me we'd have been screwed. It was a real bold move that made for an exciting passage of play.

Back in the dressing room and 35 not out, I ice my ribs, which are even more painful now, and have a meal-replacement drink along with a couple of bananas. Then Vaughany comes over and says, I want you to go out there and smash it. Play to your strengths, instinct will take over. Smash him up.

I know this is why I'm in the team instead of a batter as good as Graham Thorpe, but this is still a special situation, so it's great to hear.

We come out after lunch and Lee's at one end, Warne at the other. Lee's charging in again and I realise that even if I top-edge a hook or a pull the boundary on the leg side is so short it's going for six anyway.

I take two twos and hook a six. Warne bowls another quiet over, and then I club Lee again: two, bouncer for six, bouncer for four, full ball for four. I'm seeing it. Warne sends down another tight one to Colly, then at the end of Lee's next over, I cream successive fours, a full one crunched to the fence through mid-on and a short one to long-on.

This time, I reckon he's bowling at me in the wrong way. I'm in now, so anything short I can go at, and anything full I can drive – which I've already done on numerous occasions. He should be going back to length, sending down nicking balls – that's how I'd be bowling to myself.

But emotions are running high and everyone's super-charged: I notice Ricky Ponting at extra cover, and he's getting so frustrated he's actually calling Lee's deliveries! He's saying short, short, or pointing at his feet and telling Lee to bowl a yorker. So, although I don't predetermine, I can pre-empt, and that's pretty useful – it gets me a four through mid-on, and really helps me smash a baseball shot down the ground. Between overs, Colly tells me my eyes have gone, and I'm not surprised; I'm on another planet.

I can see the pressure's even starting to tell on Warnie. He's a lot more serious, a lot more serious than in the previous Tests. I'm not playing many shots to him or to McGrath, but then I sweep him into my boot, it balloons into the air off the ground and is caught at slip. There's an appeal and the umpires confer, but they know as well as I do: those ones are never out.

Then Warne gets Colly. Geraint Jones arrives and Shaun Tait comes on. He's got a quick, slingy action, but he's not bowled in the innings, and I crack his first two balls for four. But then, with his sixth, he gets Jones and Australia are into the bowlers. We're 199–7, 193 ahead.

Ashley Giles – or George Clooney, as I call him, because of the grey hair – comes in. We're great mates: when I was new in the team, Duncan Fletcher asked him to take me under his wing, and he really looked after me. Anything we did, he was my buddy in the side. And every time he gets bat on ball, I call out, shot, George.

In between overs Gilo and I look at the lead, check how long is left in the day and decide every time that we need to get the rate up. The aura Australia have, the reputation of the batters in their team, the way that they play – we don't even want to give them a sniff of an opportunity. They make us feel like they'd go at 8, 9, 10s an over. So we're saying, we've got to get more, we've got to get more, we've got to get more. It's unbelievably serious, and so nerve-racking.

I'm on 90, still in attack-attack-attack mode and still in my zone, as I've been for the last hour – probably since that over before lunch, in fact. Tait's very much short or full, and I'm seeing it quite slow now, picking length really well. I take him for four to midwicket, then get to 98 in singles.

In the last over before tea, Tait gives me another ball in

my area. I get forward, smack it, and as I'm following through, see the extra-cover fielder miss it. I run off in absolute glory: this is the most amazing thing that's happened to me. It's such a release. I feel light. I look up at the balcony, where the team are going mad, as if they're about to come through the window, and I want to jump up and high-five them all. I take my helmet off and raise my bat, but Gilo quietly reminds me the job isn't done yet.

The guys are absolutely buzzing in the dressing room, but I don't feel the same. I'm apprehensive, thinking, thirty overs after tea: they could chase anything. We need to grind them into the ground.

Out in the middle after the break, I keep playing Warne the way I've been playing him all series – constructively, but not recklessly. If he tosses it up, I go after it; if it's a good ball, I don't. Maybe it looks like I've decided to defend him and take on Lee and Tait, but that's purely because, at 95 or 96 mph, instinct takes over and everything seems more hectic.

It's just such an incredible feeling to be out there executing my skills against this opposition, the best in their country at what they do and some of the best in the world, but trying to outdo them. And it's exciting because I can never be totally in control: one mistake and that's it. Take it for granted and you're gone; that's what I keep telling myself.

But I know I've practised hard for these moments, against spinners on the outfield when I know it's going to kick, it's going to bounce, it's going to skid, it's going to go straight, it's going to go the other way. That's how I can enjoy the battle of it being tough like this. I'm constantly relocating myself and thinking, well, I did this okay in training the other day. I'll be able to manage here, no problem.

The best feeling on a cricket pitch is knowing that you're succeeding when the conditions are tough. I've had Shane Warne bowling on day five of the fifth Test, spinning the ball a mile, Brett Lee bowling faster than anything I've ever seen, Glenn McGrath there as well, and I've managed to get through a dodgy start and pile the pressure onto the Australians. I'm feeling extra special as a player, because every time we've needed someone to stand up, someone has stood up, and now, when we need it the most, it's my turn.

We get the rate up to 10 an over, and Gilo says, I think we have this covered now. It's the first time I really think we might be home. Then I get out to a magnificent delivery with the new ball from McGrath. I've made 158 and we're 308–8 – I'm praying that it's enough, even though it's obviously enough. I'm taking in the applause when I hear someone calling PK! PK! and Warnie comes over. Mate, you've played unbelievably well, he says. You've got to enjoy this moment. Moments like this don't come along very often, enjoy this moment, take it all in. Well done.

Walking off is just phenomenal, a crazy, out-of-body experience. I'm seeing blokes happier than I've ever seen anyone in my life and people are chanting my name, clapping me all the way up the stairs, tapping me on the back. It's the proudest feeling I've ever had.

Quite soon afterwards they got us all out, and before we came out to field Vaughany told us to put on our caps, our treasured, numbered caps. In the middle, you could see for the first time that the Aussies were human beings, and they were beaten. We bowled four balls, the umpires offered Hayden and Langer the light, they took it and the Ashes were ours.

And much as the competition was a pleasure, it's not better than when it's all over and you know you've done it. At the time, you're so focused, concentrating on the job at hand, that it's hard to enjoy it properly, but once you've conquered it it's amazing – and a lot more enjoyable than when Brett Lee's running in and bowling bouncers at you.

Since that day, people have said how I must have been thinking, Warnie's dropped the Ashes, but no – he dropped a catch, that's all, and who knows, I could have been out the next ball. Though I guess, looking back, it was a crucial moment of my life. I like to think I'd still have made it if he'd held on, but things wouldn't have gone quite the way they did.

The whole innings at the Oval was just a fantastic experience, and even now it's something Gilo and I talk about; sharing it is part of why we're still so close. I just wish I'd kept my helmet on when I celebrated, because that hairstyle is the most ridiculous hairstyle I ever had in my life. The Aussies had been calling me a granny, talking about my blue rinse, and it made me hose myself at the time, but by the Oval I'd changed it to the skunk, and it's still embarrassing to this day.

It's funny that, with such a great team as Australia were, dominating world cricket for so long, people remember them best for losing. But they know what happened in 2006/7, so I'm sure they'll take 2005's 2–1 defeat, be proud of being part of the greatest series ever and know that a year later they whitewashed us. Makes up for it, I think.

Even though I have batted to win the Ashes, the most pressure I've ever felt was playing for Surrey in 2015. It was the most mentally gruelling period of my life, because if I'd failed that would have been me done.

In my first game we played the Oxford students and, thinking about what people would say if I didn't, I simply couldn't afford not to score a century. I got 170. Then against Glamorgan I threw my wicket away in the first innings, so really had to make runs in the second, and finished 53 not out.

Against Essex, I got 32 and 8 not out. Then, the day before we played Leicestershire, my son concussed himself on his birthday. At one o'clock in the morning, I was with him while he had a CT scan, then up again at six to get back to the hospital. I almost called in to say I couldn't play, but Jess insisted that I should, so I came off the field every hour to check everything was okay.

We got them out for 292, and when I went in to bat I was incredibly nervous. People were saying it was second-division cricket, how could I get myself back into the England team this way? But in my mind, I was playing for

Surrey, my club, and the wickets weren't great. So I said to myself, I'm here to do a job. I've committed to this, everything's on the line, and I need to do well. And the only way anyone would think I'd done well was if I did something extraordinary.

A couple of their bowlers bowled brilliant first and second spells and I could have been out a few times, but I knew that if I could get through those I could score at 10 an over once I was in. It really was tough out there, which is why the next-highest score in our innings was only 36, and it took the great Kumar Sangakkara to get that.

So scoring 326 that day, and finishing 355 not out, gave me an unbelievable sense of relief. The pressure of playing at the highest level for the highest stakes is intense, but it's nothing compared to the pressure of playing for your career.

On Captaincy and Leadership

Cricket's no joke. It's a long, punishing game, physically and mentally extreme. Surprisingly, I found that when you're captain it can actually be an easier game: because I was so focused on other people, I had no time to stress about my own performances and could bat with a free spirit. But, as I also found, it can be incredibly tough.

My time leading England was brief, and it was probably right that it was, as even though I've got a good cricket brain, I just didn't understand players. When I took over from Michael Vaughan in the summer of 2008, I hadn't gone through a bad patch in my career – everything I'd touched had turned to gold. So I didn't understand the pressure that comes with failure, couldn't give sound advice and guidance and couldn't be as tolerant with people out of form as I should have been.

To be a good leader I'd also have needed to know how important families are, and how much you miss them. How amazing it is to have kids, that your kids don't care about what you score, how that joy of going home to them feels.

It's the kind of thing you think you understand even if you're single – obviously, I came from a family. But as soon as I had a proper one of my own I realised that I hadn't understood it at all, and I hadn't understood that it gives you a different perspective on life. I didn't get Steve Harmison's homesickness issues, and all I could think was, what's wrong with you? You're playing for England, you're doing everything that you're supposed to want to do. It's an absolute love of yours, and there are so many people out there who'd be willing to do it.

Then, a couple of years later, I dashed home from the World T20, we had Dylan, and then I had to go back. I wasn't mad about it – it took Jess to say, you're in the Caribbean, you should be enjoying yourself.

She was right, but it would've been much easier if she and Dylan had been there. Basically, a tour can be a bit like going on holiday without any of the people you want to go on holiday with, and even though cricketers love playing cricket, it doesn't change how important it is to be near to the people you love, and how it feels when you're not.

How difficult I found captaincy makes me realise just how

great Graeme Smith was at it. He struggled a hell of a lot at the start, being put in charge at twenty-two, taking over from a legend like Shaun Pollock, and having to control a dressing room with characters like Makhaya Ntini, Herschelle Gibbs and Mark Boucher in it. Plus he had to handle political issues that weren't there in other countries, and make sure he was fulfilling his primary obligation to the team – scoring runs. But he did it.

He had that amazing presence at the crease, which must've helped, but he's also just a nice guy. He's a very, very calm guy, and he got the best out of his players by letting them have free rein; he understood how they worked, so he knew when to push their buttons. And on his first big tour in charge, to England in 2003, he got two double centuries that united the players behind him, then stayed in the job for eleven years. Phenomenal leader, phenomenal skipper, phenomenal person.

I was twenty-eight when I was appointed, and very surprised given that I had no captaincy track record. But then there was no one else around who played in all formats of the game, so what was I going to do?

I actually started pretty well. My first game was a Test against South Africa at the Oval, a dead rubber which we won well; I scored a hundred and got Man of the Match and Man of the Series. Then, in the one-dayers, we won 4–0 and the team looked good.

One thing people commented on was that, in the field, there was a lot of physical contact between me and the guys, which I guess is how I think these things should be. I'm quite a caring bloke, and I've always felt that in the emotion of a situation, as a leader you need to show that extra special bit of attention and appreciation.

Tactically, I thought that I was fine. I understood the game of cricket well, and I was able to manoeuvre my way around from that perspective, so really I was riding high. I was playing well, and I was excited to be in charge.

But even leaving form and families aside, two other things happened that I had no real idea how to handle.

At the start of summer 2008 we played New Zealand. Between the Tests and the limited overs, a cuddly American billionaire by the name of Allen Stanford was allowed to land a black helicopter at Lord's, the home of cricket, with $20 million in a Perspex case.

Giles Clarke, then chairman of the ECB, still seemed to think that the IPL was only about money, so to compensate us for not being allowed to go and to make it seem like we didn't need to, he arranged for us to play a one-off T20 game against the Stanford SuperStars invitational XI in November. The winners would receive the coveted title of Stanford Super Series champions – and that $20 million.

Because I was captain by the time we actually had to go through with this, everything seems blurry when I look back. There was so much going on, not just with the helicopter, but with people talking about money, money, money, and guys discussing what they were going to do when they won it. I know they were just having a laugh –

Swann was quoted as saying he was going to buy himself a bright pink Ferrari – but it was all horrible, and lots of people in the media were saying so too.

So we're watching the warm-up game between Middlesex and Trinidad and Tobago, and there's cuddly Allen on the big screen, plonking Matt Prior's wife on his lap. Prior was so angry. So would I have been, if it had been my wife.

The Stanford SuperStars, alias the West Indies, absolutely pulled our pants down. They bowled us out for 99, then Chris Gayle whacked 65 from forty-five balls and we lost by ten wickets, in 12.4 overs. And, of course, cuddly Allen is now serving 110 years in prison for 'massive ongoing fraud'. Well done everyone.

But, because of that, it was actually an absolute blessing in disguise that we didn't win the game. The fact that he went down for what he went down for – goodness, if we'd each won a million dollars, imagine what the media would have said; imagine what the public would have said about the money and what we should have done. It really was a huge stroke of luck that we walked away with nothing.

Then we went to India. Before the Tests there, we played a one-day series and went 5–0 down with two to play. Not great, but India are pretty good in the format, especially at home, and I got a couple of good scores, so at least wasn't worrying about my own form. But then came the atrocities of the Mumbai attacks, in which 173 people died, and we all flew home.

Not long after, it was decided that we'd go back to play

a two-Test series, which had been the original plan – the ECB were pretty firm in insisting that its relationship with the BCCI be maintained. I didn't have any issues with the decision: I was good to go, and there was a talk from our security officer, who told us that we would get state security, government-level security. Everything would be fine.

I had to ring round all the players to explain what was going on, and what I got back were more family scenarios. I should probably have been a bit more understanding – the guys were being asked to go to a country where there'd been bombings and shootings, they had families, why would they want to leave them? If I'd had Dylan then, I would have said, fuck off, I'm not going to that place now. Finished.

But we all went. The first Test was in Chennai, where we won the toss and batted. There, sitting in the dressing room waiting to go in, I fell asleep for the first and only time in my career. But then, this was also the first and only time in my career that I'd taken a group of players home, dealt with the ECB and had to take responsibility for getting them back on tour.

I managed four runs in thirty-four balls before Zaheer Khan caught and bowled me, and then, in the second innings, Yuvraj Singh got me lbw for 1. It was the first time I'd been dismissed in both innings of a Test without reaching double figures.

Luckily, some of the others were doing okay. In our first innings Strauss made 123 and Prior 53, then Swanny and Monty took three wickets each, giving us a handy lead of 75.

When we batted again, Strauss got another ton and Colly got one too, so we set India 387 to win in just under four sessions. The highest score ever chased in India was 276 and the highest score ever chased at Chennai was 155, so we felt pretty safe.

We shouldn't have. Statistics can be misleading at the best of times, but if the chasing team has Virender Sehwag and Sachin Tendulkar batting with the most ridiculous intensity you've ever seen, it really doesn't matter what's happened before.

Sehwag spent the first over at the non-striker's end, then slammed two fours off Anderson, another two off Harmison, another one off Anderson, another two and a six off Harmison, and basically it went from there. Whatever we did, he just kept whacking it, and that's the greatness of Virender Sehwag.

At that point, my weaknesses re-emerged. Harmy kept bowling short and wide, he kept getting cut, and I lost my patience, shouting, bowl the fucking ball straight. Now, obviously, I understand the psychology of it: he's getting hit in a certain area and he knows it's because he's bowling in a certain area, but the more he's telling himself not to do it the more he's scared of doing it, and the more he can't do anything else.

I should have been helping him think positively, but I just didn't understand the pressure he was under in the middle, or the pressure he felt at being away from home. He needed a lot more encouragement, a lot more attention, and I didn't treat him in the way that I should have – the way I would have treated him after I'd had Dylan. Thinking about it now, that's clearly how Michael Vaughan got the best out of Harmy, but I didn't pick up on all that then. I was just a kid on a buzz and only interested in myself.

At one stage, Harmy didn't even want to come on to bowl, so I told Freddie that he had to keep going. Fuck off, he said. Harmy needs to bowl. I explained the situation, and he got a bit pissed off that he had to continue. It's always hot in Chennai, but it was really, really hot that day, he was knackered, and it was frustrating. We'd got ourselves into a great position to win the Test, but were now in the process of throwing it away.

That said, sometimes you just have to acknowledge the brilliance of your opponents. I always acknowledge good cricket: I love good cricket, and I think of myself as a little boy who's out there just living the dream enjoying these great players up close. Watching Sehwag take an attack apart, watching Sachin take an attack apart, watching Ponting play at Old Trafford, watching Kallis go about his business as if he's never going to get out, watching Sangakkara and Jayawardene build a partnership in Sri Lanka, watching Warnie doing what he did, watching Hayden just demoralising bowlers by hitting them over their heads in the first few overs of a Test match. These are the kinds of things that, even though you were on the receiving end, you can always look back with great fondness and say, I was lucky to have been right there.

So Viru smashed 83 off 68 balls, which took the game away from us, even though he was out before the close. We could have bowled better because we didn't bowl well, but when you analyse the situation you realise that, goodness, Sehwag was coming at us. There was a genius in the zone.

When that happens, you can bowl anywhere you want and it will still get dealt with; you've got to get him out because you can't contain him. We put in a backward point, got a third man back, but it made no difference. Anything on the stumps he was clipping, anything fourth stump he was cutting and driving. He was picking length so early that, spinning track or not, there was nothing we could do about it. We were finished.

Overnight, India were 121–1 off 29 overs, but then we got Dravid cheaply the next morning. The problem was, all that did was bring Sachin to the wicket, and he made 103 not out, batting like God. VVS didn't last long, but Yuvraj came next. Swann trapped him plumb lbw and the umpire said no; his unbeaten 85 helped get them home to the fourth-highest successful run chase in Test history. It was an interesting little twenty-four hours there.

Sometimes, though, I think that things happen for a reason. India winning and Sachin dedicating his hundred to the Mumbai victims was fate; that was just what was going to happen. And, much as I wanted it not to happen, he brought a lot of joy back to that country through the way that he, the little god of Indian cricket, won a Test match for his people. Somehow he brought a sort of stability to the country in the way that only a man as great as Sachin Tendulkar can.

In Mohali, India had the better of a draw that meant we lost the series. But I didn't feel particular pressure as I was still scoring runs – I made 144 in the first innings – and was happy with how the team was developing.

The thing was, I now had an issue with the coach, and because I wasn't happy, it's a period that I try to blot out. Mainly, I was trying to figure out how I was going to captain with this guy who, as far as I was concerned, was clearly making mistake after mistake in the way that he dealt with senior players all day every day, players who knew what they were doing.

I also thought, and still do, that the captain has to have the final say on who gets picked. It's him who's got to take the players into the middle, and if he's not comfortable with someone you're on a hiding to nothing. How can he throw the ball to a bowler he doesn't want out there? He needs to have full confidence in the XI he leads out.

I often hear people say that an international coach needs to have played international cricket, but that's wrong, though if you have there are certain mistakes you're unlikely to make. What I do I think is that an international coach needs to have been around international cricket and international cricketers for a while, so he can understand and anticipate what they need, so he can listen to them and learn from them, because that insider knowledge is essential.

Graham Ford, one of the best coaches I've ever had, never played international cricket. But when he was coach at Natal, we had Jonty Rhodes, Malcolm Marshall, Shaun Pollock and Lance Klusener on the team, guys he hung out with day in, day out. Ford's ability to make them, and others, better cricketers was something he developed over a good number of years before becoming South Africa coach.

Or look at a guy like Trevor Bayliss. Never played for Australia, but coached New South Wales for years before he was appointed by Sri Lanka. Then he went to the Big Bash and the IPL, and all that will help him do a good job for England.

At the top of the game, players are pretty good – they've got to be, to get themselves there. What you need to create as leader of an international cricket team is an environment that is caring and chilled out, where people feel special. That's how you get the best out of them. So that's what coaching needs to focus on, but instead there are all these qualifications – levels that guys have to pass, from one to four.

If you've played international cricket for a number of years you understand the game. You just do. The thing that you need to study, understand and figure out is man-management, so if you go down the path of coaching you need a lecture or two and a class or two, because that stuff is fundamental.

But goodness, this arrangement where it takes you two

years to get a level-four coaching badge even if you've played a hundred Test matches is ridiculous.

I'm pretty sure that Darren Lehmann's not got any of these qualifications, and he's brilliant, nor Gary Kirsten, nor Duncan Fletcher, who led England to Ashes glory and did brilliantly with India. I don't see all the great coaches sitting around polishing their wonderful level-four badges, and that's why I think it's a dangerous place that cricket is going to.

Obviously it's not just about being looked after – sometimes players need technical help. But I don't think the coach needs to have complete control over that. If I were a coach I'd let each player bring his own guy in, if that was what he wanted; if I couldn't help, he could have his own guy throw to him and get him right to score me runs.

I'd want everybody to buy into the philosophy that I think you need to be successful: hard work and hard training, but a very relaxed atmosphere where players can come in and have an unbelievably good time. You respect your teammates, so you're punctual for everything that gets put on, but otherwise it's the job of the coach to take the pressure off. He needs to manage expectations so that people achieve what they should be achieving, not set silly targets for certain individuals to make them feel that the success of the team is entirely down to them.

The other position that needs to be seriously considered, and which must be filled by a strong, powerful character, is the academy director. You need to have somebody who youngsters look up to and want to learn from. It's not a position in which they can afford to have someone people take the piss out of. It's not right. It shouldn't be like that.

I was very fortunate to have Rod Marsh looking after me when I was at Loughborough, and then on tour in India with the Lions. Every day I got to meet and speak to Rod, understand how he went about his business, and think, wow, this guy's an Australian legend – I can learn so much from him.

Rod brought the experience of what's required to play in international cricket. You could ask him what you needed to do to make it and he would tell you: you need to be hard-working, you need to be tough, you need to be able to cut and pull. He was brilliant.

The one particular thing I remember him saying was how we needed to be able to play the short ball. So we used to practise it in the indoor school: we had guys like Simon Jones and Sajid Mahmood running in at us, bowling bouncers at 90 mph, and some of us wondered what we were being made to do it for. Then he'd come downstairs, watch the practice and say, listen, you better get on with this, because if you go to Australia, if you play in an Ashes battle, you'll have Brett Lee trying to knock your head off. This is where you practise to become good at it. So that was something that I definitely took from him.

But Rod Marsh wasn't great just because he was Rod Marsh. He also instilled a serious training ethic and took very good care of us. He was really tough in the nets, but you could go and speak to him afterwards, and then in the evenings he was magnificent. Seven o'clock, he'd always be in the bar to buy the lads a beer, and you'd just talk cricket, go through old times, talk about your game, talk about improvements. A great man, Rodders.

At the same time, the first team had Duncan Fletcher, another magnificent coach and human being. Fletch understood me and gave me free rein. He knew that I was a free spirit and he encouraged me to be myself. And that's exactly what Michael Vaughan did as well.

Vaughan's attitude in the middle, as well as the dressing room, was infectious. You never really knew whether he was in good form or bad form, he just played. He was a calm person who went about things in a very mature way, and quietly achieved what he achieved – Joe Root reminds me a little of him.

What was great about Vaughan, apart from his feel for the game, was the way that he commanded a dressing room with more stubborn and fiery characters than the one I was in later on that got out of hand. It was probably the only team I've played in where there weren't really any issues in the side and the guys all got on with each other, which I think was purely because of how good the man-management was. Everybody was treated how they wanted to be treated and there was no pressure.

In particular, Vaughany captained Freddie real well, because he could be difficult; he's a free spirit, so training sessions and team meetings were not always things that he wanted to do. Vaughan simply adapted, and included Freddie in his core of senior players who ran the team, along with Hoggard, Trescothick, Harmison and Geraint Jones.

Usually, they'd get together five or ten minutes before the rest of us met and then, before we'd discuss the opposition, they would give us their insights into the game we had coming up and see if there was anything to check up on. Is training okay? Is there anything we need to do to get better? Then, if there was an overwhelming vote about something that we were doing wrong, or something that we were doing well, they would re-emphasise it and make sure everyone knew what was what. And you've also got to give credit to Fletcher for allowing those guys to just get on with it.

He knew that we were all there to work hard, and I always appreciated him recognising that in me – he even wrote about it in his book. He knew how much I wanted to be successful, he knew that I was very respectful in everything that I did, and that I was very, very professional. It's something that, with all the bullshit that's gone on over the last few years, a lot of people have probably forgotten about me. My professionalism has never, ever, ever wavered.

I was invited onto that players' management committee a year into my international career, and that involvement made it even clearer to me that it's a great way to lead. You've got all your key players with you, you're benefiting from their experience, and the responsibility encourages them to contribute more.

In my short spell as captain, I'd go to Straussy and Colly

for all those reasons, but I quickly realised that I should talk to everybody because you can learn from anybody. I don't care if you've played no Test matches or a hundred Test matches, because a guy who's played a hundred Test matches has probably forgotten something that a guy that hasn't played a single Test has fresh in his mind.

During the 2015 CPL, before a game, I mentioned to a young teammate that it'd be a real strong shot to hit through midwicket. But he told me that, because the pitch was quite slow, he was finding it hard; it took a guy who hadn't played much cricket to bring up a simple point that made me realise conditions weren't as safe as I thought.

The more I've played, the more I've realised that the environment created by the captain and coaches is possibly the most important part of their roles. These days there's extreme pressure on international sportsmen – more than ever before. Anybody with a mobile phone is a journalist, anybody can take a picture of you or tweet something about you. Your life is on everybody's mobile phone, your life is on everybody's television.

And Test cricket, while wonderful, is also stressful. You're away for a long time and the games go on for a long time. So actually, team environments shouldn't just be relaxed, they should be the most relaxed environments that players go into, where their talents are nurtured and no one's fussing about consequences. An environment in which coaches are constantly putting pressure on and checking them out all the time is pointless, and so is having too many rules. Clearly, if you don't respect your privilege you're going to get found out, but there's never much of that. Everyone wants it too much.

One of the fantastic things I saw during England's series against New Zealand in 2015 was that Paul Farbrace, the coach at the time, wasn't sitting on the balcony with a notepad. He was sitting there with a smile on his face, laughing and joking with the players and listening to the commentary. When you've got a coach like that, it's refreshing. Duncan Fletcher was slightly different, but also amazing: during matches, he used to sit behind the computer straight-faced, but in the dressing room he'd be laughing and joking. And that's what you want.

All the reports I hear about Darren Lehmann are that he's the most easy-going bloke. Don't mess him about, don't go and get drunk and do something stupid that brings the game into disrepute, but enjoy doing your job. Have dinner, have a beer, have a bottle of wine, celebrate if you win – just do your job. Don't feel like you're going to be monitored.

Sportsmen don't need to be monitored. These days, in some teams there are more backroom staff than players: psychologists, doctors, all those things. You do not need that many people travelling with you. You need a coach, you need a manager, you need a physio, you need a masseur – but that's it. Doctors are everywhere, so use a local one if you need to; you don't need psychologists on tour because you can do sessions on Skype or FaceTime.

Then you've got a bowling coach, you've got a fielding coach, you've got a batting coach, you've got an assistant coach, you've got a coach. Just have a coach. Your head coach should be responsible for either bowling or batting; take someone to be in charge of the other discipline if you want, and that's enough. There are too many people walking around, hanging about and taking up space on the bus. There are too many people with opinions, there's too much technology, there are too many theories. Just get your team together, get a solid base, give people security.

I can't overstate how important security is, in every respect. Take Ravi Bopara, for example. He's a properly gifted player and the selectors must know it, because they've picked him so many times. He's maturing, improving and he gets into the IPL, which says a lot – you don't see many other English guys in there.

But, in my opinion, he's always been treated unfairly in terms of security. He's been moved up and down the order and never given the confidence that comes with having a run in the team – he's never played more than six Tests in a row, when you need at least ten. He'd do well, badly, well, badly, and no one ever said to him, okay, you're my number five – go out there and do the business for me for six months. It took Kallis ten innings to get a Test century, he didn't get another until his twenty-sixth, and in all that time he only got two fifties. It took Steve Waugh forty-two Test innings to get a century. Sometimes with talent, you need to persevere.

The wider point is that you have to understand the needs of all the people you captain and coach. Every team is full of different characters, and it's how you manage them, how you manage the ones who don't have confidence, how you bring them out, how you keep others on an even keel, how you help them through their ups and downs, that shows how good a leader you are.

Team bonding falls within this. We had a massive night out when we arrived in Australia for the 2011/12 series and it was legendary within the team. Not as great a memory as all the success that came after, but still a significant part of it.

So when we arrived in Perth in 2013, the guys were looking forward to doing it again, and it's those times when you bond, take the piss out of each other, bring the new players out of themselves and get new nicknames. Everyone has it with their group of mates, and it helps you stick together when things get tough. I'm not a big drinker at all, but I'm a great believer in building team spirit by all going out together. It's a shame we weren't allowed to do it on that tour as I think it would have benefited us all enormously.

Everyone needs to be treated as an individual, whether they're young or old – you shouldn't have to earn it. Just look at Ben Stokes. You pick him because he's a free spirit, you want him to play like a free spirit, but then if you're deliberately hard on him how's that supposed to work? Now that his spirit is being recognised, he's performing properly.

*

Man-management is a vital aspect of leadership and something that Straussy could be very good at. All you need to do is read and listen to what the other players say about him to know that. Admittedly we failed together at times, which I think he'd acknowledge, but we had some great times too.

In particular, he managed his bowlers really well and gave them a lot of freedom. In turn, they delivered more often than not. One area in which we could have done better, though, is that the most of the time the bowlers would decide on the plans we'd use to attack the opposition. Batters, being batters, understand batting. They know what the difficulties are, and they know where the weaknesses are.

During this time we were very fortunate to have Graeme Swann in the team, because Straussy could just bring him on at any time and he'd make something happen. That's what Alastair Cook has missed in the last couple of years, and he's still missing it now. His biggest issue was never going to be my non-selection, but the inability to bring on a world-class spinner to get him wickets and cover for his lack of inspiration.

Someone like Ricky Ponting was a forceful and dominant kind of guy and this transferred through to his captaincy. Although there were reservations about him strategically, he led a team that absolutely annihilated the competition. They were ruthless.

Graeme Smith was another, very unconventional in how

he played, but he punished attacks and captained in that style.

In the end, tactics is thinking; you think how you are, you are how you bat, and taking Cook, for example, he's a pragmatic and diligent kind of batter.

If you watched us under Cooky and Straussy, you'd have seen that when players like Smith, Jayawardene and Sangakkara got in, there was the danger that was it. And of course I know that they were, and in Sangakkara's case still are, great players. But when that happens you perhaps need someone with the know-how to sneak them out; you need to think outside the box, and there are only a few people around able to do that.

It's not necessarily about charisma, or even being an unconventional kind of person – just an unconventional kind of player. That's how you understand what people's weak points are, and when you should go straight to Plan B. It's the ability to look at the world differently, anticipate things and be brave, and that's guys like Brendon McCullum, Michael Vaughan, Misbah-ul-Haq, Michael Clarke and Virat Kohli.

Even during the 2015 Ashes, when Cooky did pretty well, you could see it was a problem at times. Before the first Test, England planned their lines and fields perfectly and the bowlers delivered, but in the second Test things went badly wrong from day one. When good players get in on a flat wicket, you need to create things to get them out. That's when you need a spark, that's when you need to be inventive and spontaneous. But instead, England kept at it with the same outside of off-stump line to Steve Smith and he made 215.

What Cook does have in abundance is the ability to lead from the front, which I'd argue is the most important attribute a captain needs. If you're playing well you'll be buzzing, and so will the players. On top of that, it means you're understanding conditions and have more confidence in your judgement, so you become a lot more daring and a lot smarter with the tactical decisions you make.

From a technical aspect, brilliant coaches are the ones who recognise a problem in your batting, bowling or whatever, then give you the tools so you can fix it. Take my form in the summer of 2000, for example. I was struggling and left out of the ODI squad ahead of a big Ashes series Australia. I went to see Graham Ford and he fixed me immediately; two months later I scored a double hundred in Adelaide. It meant so much to me, and I can't thank Fordy enough. That's why, whenever I've had the opportunity to play for Surrey, I've played for them: I love Graham Ford. And that's what coaching is about.

It also, to my mind, emphasised how important the training methods for younger players are. Steve Finn, for example, is a lovely, fun guy, but he needs confidence, and that comes from experience.

In Hobart, before our first warm-up game against Australia A in 2013, I saw him down in the nets. Finny, get your spikes on, come and bowl, I said.

I'm not allowed to.

What do you mean, not allowed to?

I'm not allowed to bowl.

Are you kidding me? Get your spikes on and come bowl, I want to face you, I want you to get better, I'll help you and you can help me by bowling to me.

No, I've got to keep my trainers on and I've got to visualise bowling. I've got to think about bowling and I've got to go through the motions of bowling.

Somebody who bowls at 90 miles an hour shouldn't be talking technique, or even thinking about it, he should just be bowling and bowling and bowling. That, as far as I am concerned, is the only way he will get confident.

Then once the series got under way, we had a petrified lower order being told to score runs, but no one showing them how to do it – just getting shouted at when they got out in the nets, being asked what they thought they were playing at. So in Alice Springs, I spent time with Broady, Jimmy and Tremlett, throwing balls at them for hours, trying to give them a method to defend fast bowling. Broad's a tall guy, so doesn't need to move his feet too much, and Anderson's super-talented with great hand–eye coordination. I taught them a trigger, had them looking for the ball and just tried to build their confidence so that they didn't struggle as much in the middle. We can all help each other in these situations and the best leaders are those who use every tool at their disposal.

On Conditions

Test-match wickets should be flat. It's called Test cricket for a reason, and that isn't because it's the easiest job in the world.

You want a bit in the pitch on the first morning, but after that only the bowler who bends his back and has the ability to do the business should do the business. Then, through days three, four and five it should deteriorate and start spinning, so that by the end it's not a minefield, but it's close to a minefield. That way, only the best players with the best techniques survive, you get results and you get great games. Flat wickets are also called good wickets for a reason.

Whatever people say, no wicket is ever truly flat, just as no wicket is ever too flat. What they mean is that batsmen have batted well and bowlers have bowled badly. There's swing, reverse swing, seam, spin – you can find something on anything, and people get out in all kind of favourable circumstances. I've never gone anywhere in the world and thought, we will never get out on this. It's just so easily done. You get low scores on good pitches, and sometimes they lull you into a false sense of security. People say, how the hell have I done that? I can't believe I did that. Well, you did.

It's true that if the pitch is good, it's helpful to bat first – and bowl last – which makes the toss, and luck, important. But it's not decisive, because there are still five days to go; you just have to work it out. First-innings runs are important whenever you make them and wickets don't crumble so fast that they're the flattest thing in the world on day one but an absolute danger on day three. You simply have to handle the scoreboard pressure.

Of all the Tests played that have finished in a positive result, only 53 per cent have been won by the side winning the toss, which tells you that it's an advantage but not a decisive one. If it goes your way you still have to perform, and if it doesn't there's still plenty of time to impose your skills.

Even though the team batting first might get the best of the batting conditions, the team bowling first might still get the best of the bowling conditions. Other times, teams might just misread the pitch, which is why 'good toss to lose' is a cliché – we saw that in the third Ashes Test of 2015, when Alastair Cook wanted to bat, Michael Clarke did bat, and Australia were rolled for 136.

For that reason, I'm not like Shane Warne, who says 'Bat bat bat bat bat bat' if you win the toss. If you field, you might be able to get ten wickets on day one – that's how many you'd need to make it the right call – and sometimes the best batting conditions come on days two and three, especially if the sun comes out. And actually, teams who've won the toss and fielded have won 38 per cent of the time, whereas teams who've won the toss and batted have won 28 per cent of the time.

Usually, you'd only put a team in in England or New Zealand, when grass on the wicket and overcast skies mean you know the ball's going to seam and swing more. In Australia, where it tends to be clear and sunny and beautiful, the Kookaburra ball only goes for a few overs and the wickets are flat with good bounce, you bat. In South Africa, the same. In the West Indies, you bat because the wickets are flat. In India you bat because the wickets are flat until they start spinning. But none of that means you can't get people out, and within all these countries different grounds have different quirks.

At Headingley, for example, when there's cloud cover there's movement through the air and off the pitch; otherwise it's an absolute road and it doesn't seam at all. And whatever's going on with the weather, you've got to bowl full.

A lot of fast bowlers come to England and think that their southern-hemisphere lengths will work fine. But actually, because the wickets aren't conducive to pace, you've got to get the ball up to the batsman – not too full, but just full of a length, giving the ball time to swing and making sure that they can't just watch it onto the bat once it's bounced. You'll probably take some damage doing it and get punished through the covers a couple of times, but who wouldn't take an average of eight? Drive for four, drive for four, *snick*.

Guys like McGrath, Steyn, Pollock, Asif, Wasim Akram, Tim Southee and Trent Boult got to grips with that – even Ambrose and Walsh went fuller. But Morkel still hasn't and Lee never did. And not only do you have to be patient in England, but you can afford to be: the Duke ball does more once the lacquer comes off, and then it goes all day.

Pitchwise, what you want in England is a bit of assistance for the fast bowlers early on – some sort of colour and texture, but not over-grassy or over-green. That gives you good, even bounce to encourage strokeplay, but slips and gully are also in the game.

Until 2013 or so, most wickets in England were a version of this: not too fast, not too slow, not too low, not too bad. Just a beautiful pace for entertaining, not attritional, cricket. Since then, the drainage has killed a lot of them. Or at least that's how it seems to me, though I'm no expert, and I know that some groundsmen think differently.

Either way, there've been too many poor Test tracks in recent years. Bouncers have been useless because the ball just sits up, and on the first morning keepers have caught on the bounce and captains have been forced to set straight fields because there's no carry to third slip and gully. Flat wickets, yes; dead wickets, no.

Although the weather in the week leading up to the game might have had an effect, we saw a pitch like that at Lord's in the 2015 Ashes – at least for the first two days, until the sun quickened it up a bit. Usually, though, Lord's is like Headingley: you look up, not down, and after a run of six consecutive draws between 2006 and 2008 there have been only two since, so they're doing something right.

And what you always get at Lord's is the tradition and complete amazingness of the place. You just feel so lucky every time you get selected to play there, because of how much you can feel the history, because of all the greats who have played there.

Lord's has got a very respectful sort of calming hum around the ground, a murmur that's purely conversation. They clap good shots whoever plays them and they applaud good innings and good catches. It's not a hostile environment like the other English grounds, and I think it encourages the opposition to up their game – they know that they're going to have a week off from the direct abuse they get everywhere else around the country.

The other thing about playing at Lord's is that the lunches are not to be missed. They are just very, very special. You've got a full-on selection like in a restaurant, with a choice of starters, three or four main courses, dessert options and table service. If you're batting, then obviously you miss out, but if you're done or if you're fielding you take it on – especially the prawns in hollandaise sauce they have on the table to start you off. Those are taken apart by the lads as soon as they get up there; they always get absolutely destroyed.

If I was putting together my ideal five-match tour of England, Headingley and Lord's would be there, but Old Trafford wouldn't. I know lots of batters enjoy it, but I never have. I didn't go well there, and even though I got a century there once they turned the strip around I still don't like the look of it. It's very patchy, with bits of grass and bits of dryness, so although it plays okay, whenever you look down at it, it never looks like it's a good wicket. It doesn't fill me with confidence; it doesn't make me feel, oh yeah, this is an absolute ripper, it's a beauty.

So I'd go with the Oval, where the track encourages positive cricket; Edgbaston, because the crowd and conditions are great; and the Rose Bowl, which I think is the best English pitch – the one we played Sri Lanka on in 2011 was an absolute belter. Consistent bounce, bounce for the spinners and you could play good cricket shots on it; that's how it's meant to be.

For similar reasons, my favourite ground in Australia is Adelaide. Obviously I got runs there, so I'm biased, but I always found the track fair and evenly paced – magnificent to bat on with no swing or seam, before deteriorating to keep low and take spin.

These days the pitch is a drop-in, but I don't know what it does, because when I played on it Mitchell Johnson ruined us with 7–40. It used to be quick enough for the batters to play strokes on, but not so quick that bowlers tear you apart, and even though we got torn apart that's probably still the case. Johnson was just that good.

In general, the fast, bouncy Australian wickets are all really good for batting and I've got no issue with that at all. You've got to adjust your game, so it can take you a bit longer to get in, and it's really important to leave well, because a lot more balls are going over the stumps, but that's what you want. You want a different challenge.

Home advantage is part of the game, and a great part of the game; going somewhere unfamiliar, where you've got to adapt, tests you physically and mentally. It forces you to understand your game better, to become a better player, and makes for better cricket.

But there are other challenges of playing in Australia, particularly if you're English.

Australians are brought up to be fierce competitors – that's why their teams are so good. Being a fiery character myself, I'm fine with that. If I'm confronted, I'll stand up, fight my corner, and won't back down. Australians don't back down either.

During away Ashes series I've been abused a lot, but that was just the way they went about me, and I totally understood. It was like Ricky Ponting or Shane Warne in England. Our supporters smashed them because they were targeting the player they thought most threatened their chances of winning.

But people constantly trying to intimidate you and insult you – every time you get into a taxi, for example – can get a bit much. When we got beaten 5–0 in 2006/7, I went to dinner with my wife and the driver started singing songs about how shit the English were. And not in a friendly way at all; he properly wanted to get at us. In the end, Jess pointed out that we were paying him for a service and asked him to be a bit more respectful, but she really shouldn't have had to.

Another time, I was in a restaurant with my whole family, and some random guy says, I hope you get fucked up tomorrow, you white kaffir. Seriously. And in the hotel, a cleaning lady once asked one of the guys' wives, are you one of the kept women?

You also get some severe things said when you're on the boundary, along with the light relief of 'KP's a wanker' and 'You're a wanker'. You get called a wanker all day every day.

And I enjoyed it sometimes, but other times I didn't – it can grind you down. But the amazing thing is that now, because of the Big Bash, my time in Australia is great. I love the country.

Another ground I particularly enjoy is Newlands in South Africa. It's so beautifully picturesque, and it's great sitting in the dressing room with Table Mountain just there, same as when you're standing in the field looking at it.

Kingsmead in Durban is also special to me. I played my first first-class game and my first fifty-over domestic game there – it's home, so it's always a thrill to go back and play.

And then there's Johannesburg and Centurion, which are in the Highveld. The air is thinner up there, so the ball travels faster through it; scoring rates are faster, it's easier to hit boundaries and you get full value for the big shots you play. But, more or less, conditions are similar to those in Australia.

In India, my favourite ground is the Feroz Shah Kotla in Delhi. The wicket is evenly paced, very flat, and very good for batting, but it's really all about the atmosphere, which is incredible. Having your name chanted by forty thousand people as soon as you walk out to the middle is a special feeling, and I feel at home whenever I play there.

Every time I go abroad, I try to embrace the local culture. I learned early in my career to always eat the local food because that's what they're best at making, but it helps you feel settled in a place as well. When we went to India in 2012, a few of the guys were really worried about spending so long there, so I tried my hardest to get them out by organising things for us to do – only trips to restaurants, bars and cinemas, but enough to show that there's a little bit more to the country than hotel rooms and playing FIFA. And, though I'm not claiming any credit, we were relaxed, we had fun and we came from behind to win easily – not something that happens often on the subcontinent.

Like India, Sri Lanka is a wonderful country with wonderful people. They love their cricket, they're really kind and generous, and not at all intrusive. But because it's a little island in the ocean, the humidity is death, it's a joke. It just hits you like you've walked into a wall.

That's why, in my opinion, the 151 I made in Colombo

in 2012 was my best Test innings. It was 45° and 100 per cent humidity, and I struggle badly in those conditions.

I've always been really fit, and pride myself on my conditioning, but the temperature there is out of control. In some training sessions I'd lose four or five kilos, and every single morning I'd wake up, go downstairs and drink a litre of coconut water. But it was still impossible.

The heat was at its worst out in the middle. Ideally, I'd have taken my helmet off, but the way that I play means I can't, even against spinners. As I sweep and reverse-sweep there's always a chance I might top-edge into my face, and I also like to get my head as near to the ball as possible, so don't feel confident batting without protection.

That tour was the only time I took nine pairs of gloves with me, because I knew that if I was going to bat for any length of time I'd have to be changing them a lot. I also took inners, because I'm a ridiculous sweater and get unbelievably sweaty hands, so decided I'd try them; after my first net session I threw them all away. Being a feel player, they just didn't work for me; I need to be as close as possible to the grip of the bat, not to have the leather of the gloves, plus the inner, in between. So that was that, and my hands had to cope.

During the first Test in Galle I seriously irritated myself getting out to Chanaka Welegedara by not lining up his left-arm seam properly. I was standing on leg stump as usual, and when he came around the wicket I maintained my position, which meant that I wasn't quite sure where my off stump was.

It was just a little mistake; I should have gone over to middle, because then I would have triggered onto off. Any ball outside my right eye I could've left, whereas the way it was, any ball outside my right eye was bowling me, which meant I was in no man's land.

After that day's play I went to the nets and worked really hard with Mushy, cross that I made such a silly error. I got myself right, went out in the second innings and lined Welegedara up beautifully. Although Suraj Randiv had me caught for 30 and we ended up losing, I felt like my game was in really good shape.

Then we travelled up to Colombo, and just before the Test I had one of the most amazing practices I've ever had – the spinners were bowling, I middled everything and I was picking areas to hit. I was saying to myself, over extra cover, and *bang*, I'd whack over extra cover. Right, sweep this ball, and *bang*, I'd sweep it. I only batted for twenty minutes, but it was such a good little session.

The standard of net bowlers on the subcontinent is pretty high; they all have some mystery about them, and not just because you don't know who they are. Some are good wrist spinners and some are good doosra bowlers, so they really test you. One of my favourite things about touring Asia is just saying, okay guys, you've got to get me out here – you've got ten minutes to get me out. They try so hard to do it that you've got to be right on your game, especially because the practice tracks aren't as good as the ones you get for Tests, which makes it a really good workout.

So that's what I did next. We went into a different net and after ten minutes I walked out of there on cloud nine. I was choosing where to hit every single ball, I was hitting 360, I was sweeping, I was reverse-sweeping, I was slog-sweeping, I was driving, I was defending, I was nudging, I was hitting it over cover, I was hitting the ball straight. I went through a full array of shots and left saying, if I get myself in tomorrow, for the first time I can feel confident of getting a big score in Colombo.

I actually had to wait a bit longer, because Sri Lanka won the toss and batted. Mahela made his second first-innings hundred of the series, and we bowled them out for 275 – not a terrible score on that ground.

We started well in reply, but were scoring pretty slowly. Straussy made 61, Cook 94, and when I went in at 213–2 Trotty was 54 not out.

Whenever you start an innings you're sweating, your heart's racing and your mouth's dry with nerves, but with the temperature that morning it was something else. My head was thumping, pulsing and vibrating like it was going to explode and burst my helmet, which felt like the heaviest thing in the world.

Usually, people talk about red mist and they mean a state of anger, but you get it in heat like that as well. The more you dehydrate, the more there's this haze in your brain, and occasionally it blurs your vision.

I knew that if I wanted to be successful I'd have to score really, really quickly. And that's what I did. It was just a case of finding my zone from practice again, so I made a decision to be super-positive, super-aggressive and super-destructive. I was playing spin beautifully and the boundaries were short, especially straight, so I backed myself to mis-hit sixes – not something I always do, but that day I was sure I could. Anything that I thought I could hit over the fence, I hit over the fence.

When Tillakaratne Dilshan stopped his run-up a couple of times, saying I'd moved to reverse-sweep him too early; I was warned for timewasting, but I hardly even noticed, and that was the funny thing about that innings: there was nothing to notice. My other best knocks, there are shots people remember – off Steyn, Ojha, Murali, Lee, Warne, all those guys. But this one, it was just me trusting my ability to do everything I knew I could do, doing it, and having the gloves to back it up; I went through all nine pairs, and four shirts.

I guess the speed I scored at changed the course of that game; 151 in a session and a half. It's what Mahela and Graham Ford, who was coaching Sri Lanka at the time, always say: they would have won that series if it wasn't for me. And, as I've said before, it makes a big difference to how you feel about an innings when it helps your team get a win.

But the reason why I rank it as my best isn't anything I did technically, but rather how demanding it was, both physically and mentally. That's why I celebrated so much when I got to my 150. I'd always thought it was impossible for me, but I found a way.

Second in my mind is the Oval in 2005, because of the enormity of the occasion, the bowling attack that I faced and it being my first Test hundred. Then at three is the 227 I hit against Australia at Adelaide in 2010, which came off a long drought of not making a hundred. I'd gone through a lot to get my form back, so the release was something I'll never forget. Four would be the century I scored in my first Test innings against South Africa in 2008, which was just something that was really special to me, especially because of the reception that I got – probably the most emotional, appreciative applause that I got in my career. And then at five is the Mumbai 186. Even though it was quite hard to get out, conditions weren't batsman-friendly, the ball was spinning a mile and it needed a lot of intelligence and technical ability not to succumb that day, and also to score as quickly as I did.

On the Best

I've talked a lot about the players I respect and the methods that made them successful, so I wanted to put together my dream team. The rule is that I need to have played Test cricket either with or against them, so before I start, it's important to make clear that I only ever came across the great Brian Lara in one-day internationals. I had the unbelievable privilege of watching him up close then, but never over the longer format.

1. Virender Sehwag

Just an incredibly positive cricketer, the kind of cricketer who can win a Test match in a session or two – on song, he was just an absolute superstar. If you didn't get him out very, very early, he'd destroy you.

He played Test cricket in the same way he does limited overs: lots of cuts, dives and slashes, looking to hit every ball to the boundary. He plays spinners superbly, and is generally extremely dismissive of slow bowling.

But, whatever pace he's facing, he'll look to dominate anything in his half, and anything on fourth or fifth stump means a cut shot, because to Sehwag that's width. Our plan against him was always to go at or just over his stumps, cramp his style and bring in all forms of dismissal; sometimes it worked, sometimes it didn't. His innings at Chennai in 2008 was one of the best I've ever seen, and he also scored 319 off 304 balls against Steyn, Morkel, Ntini, Kallis and Paul Harris, which is frankly ridiculous.

Technically, he's really sound. He plays beautifully through the off side and his hands and eyes are phenomenal, but what's key are the positions he gets into with his head; they're magnificent.

What I mean by that is that he's always very close to the ball. He doesn't use big foot movements at all and plays pretty much on the crease, but because he watches so well he's always in a great position to get his hands through the shot. He's got really strong wrists that help him generate so much power.

And yet, he's not really a power player. His bats are pretty light, but freakish hand–eye coordination gives him beautiful timing. That's how he generates such speed through the ball, and that's what gets him his runs.

What's also incredible about Viru is his confidence. When he arrives at the ground he never looks at the wicket, because it makes no difference to him; he's going to play his game, and that's the end of it.

Away from cricket, Sehwag is exactly as you'd expect. Chilled out, carefree, a free spirit and a wonderful bloke who's always looking for the positive options in life. He's just a really, really top man.

2. Sachin Tendulkar

A genius and a superstar. Like the best players in any sport, he seemed to have a lot more time to do his thing than everyone else, and he was amazingly consistent.

He also had absolutely astonishing mental strength. The weight of expectation on his shoulders and on his wicket every single time he walked out to play for India, and the way he handled it, makes him an even greater player and an even greater bloke in my eyes.

I remember in 2004, he'd got out nicking off a few times because Australia were bowling full and wide at him, so for the fourth Test at the SCG he decided he was going to put his cover drive away. Somehow, he actually managed to go a full ten hours at the crease without playing it; in his 241 not out, the third of his six Test double centuries, there was only one boundary in front of square on the off side. Just to be able to say to yourself, I'm not going to do something for a day or two because it's becoming a bit of a weakness, when it actually wasn't a weakness, and then turn up and still get a huge score – it's impossible to understand how that's possible, it's freak-of-nature stuff.

Sachin always played brilliantly correct cricket, getting into wonderful positions and driving the ball straight down the ground. I guess he was a front-foot player, unless he fancied playing on the back foot. His technique was fairly orthodox, and he didn't do anything silly, but as soon as you strayed anywhere near his pads he would punish you through the leg side.

Against short stuff, he just got out of the way, but when you pick length as well as he did, you go okay. And obviously he murdered spinners, Shane Warne included, with magnificent foot movement, forwards and backwards.

Basically, he would look to get in and intend to take the game away from you at some stage – but to start with, he wanted to bat time. While he was doing that he'd still score at a decent rate, and he took that ability into fifty- and twenty-over cricket. I might be picking these guys for a fantasy Test team, but they're all really good at limited overs as well. They're all just really good.

That's why I've got Sachin in as an opener. He did the job in the shorter forms, and he's a great enough player to adapt. Having him in any side puts fear into the opposition, and if he's together with Sehwag it's even more formidable. Bowlers would know that they were going to be attacked.

Although Sachin is small, he isn't at all slight, and his

small, strong wrists and strong arms meant that he could use a very, very heavy bat. That allowed him to lean on deliveries; as soon as he hit the ball it was going to start talking. He was just an unbelievably special player, and when Warne says that you weren't only the best, but you were noticeably better than Lara, that's an incredible tribute.

By the time I played against Sachin, we had a plan for him, and we always felt that we could bowl to him. But if you speak to the guys who played against him five and ten years earlier, the likes of Warne and McGrath, they'll tell you that on some days there was absolutely no way you could bowl to him at all; he just demolished you. What happens is that as you go deeper into your thirties your eyes deteriorate, but even as that happened he still found a way, and ended up with a hundred international hundreds. What a legend.

Off the field, Sachin is another wonderful guy, very hospitable, very caring and very generous with his time. A remarkable man.

3. Ricky Ponting

If you look at the all-time top twenty run-scorers in Test cricket, only three of them spent most of their career batting at number three – Dravid and Sangakkara are the other two. Maybe it's a coincidence, or maybe it's because number three is the hardest position to bat, because you need to be able to defend and attack. With Ricky Ponting, second in the all-time list behind Sachin, it was mainly the latter.

He was incredibly aggressive, there to punish you, and brilliant off both front foot and back foot; the positions he got into when playing the pull shot or the drive down the ground were like a boxer in full flow. Ponting was probably the only player I played against who was an absolute master yet didn't have a trigger, just a forward press. He had such incredible eyes, such incredible hands and such incredible hand–eye coordination that he could be dominant and powerful without needing to get set first, which takes amazing reaction speed.

The reason he could make that work was because his head position was still great, really close to the ball, and he was also very strong, especially in the forearms. The viciousness of his strokeplay created energy in the middle, inspired his teammates and intimidated bowlers. Against him, their margin for error was tiny, and if they got him on one of his many days they were done. Anything full of a length got driven, anything short of a length got pulled, anything that bounced high enough he hooked, and he cut the shit out of you.

Our plan for him was to attack the stumps, to try to get him out lbw. Because he committed so early on his press, sometimes, at the start of his innings, you could drag his front foot across the stumps and he'd be falling over. Then you could get him lbw, nick him off or, if he missed it, have him clean-bowled.

If you bowled short to him you had to bowl really short, not between chest and neck, but above the eyes or in line with them above the shoulder, because you can't properly control balls above and outside the eyeline. Otherwise, he'd just dismiss you. And though the margin for error was small, it was something to try, to turn a strength into a weakness, because with players as good as him, sometimes that's all you've got.

Once he was there or thereabouts, if he was picking length and not just planting his foot, you were dead. If you had the misfortune to face him in those circumstances, as we did on so many occasions, the only thing you could do was try to frustrate him. On occasion, we'd try to starve him of the strike, but the main thing was to keep him playing with a straight bat: as soon as you fed his main strengths, the cuts and the pull, you were in even worse trouble than before.

The best batter of my generation.

4. Jacques Kallis

Gun. Machine. Before England played South Africa in 2008, we had a team meeting in which we talked about Kallis, his batting and how great he was. Then we got to the bit where we had to work out a plan for getting him out, couldn't think of one, so decided, in all seriousness, that he was a run-out candidate early in his innings. He was just that technically sound and solid in defence that we couldn't find anything else to go on, and in the 2004/5 series they'd got him that way in Cape Town – though not until he'd made 66. It was a struggle the rest of the time, too: he scored three hundreds in five matches, at an average of 69.44.

What was also great about Kallis was his pacing. He could just bat all day doing the same thing, and was always looking to occupy the crease, playing smart cricket that meant you got hardly any chances. He left well, he played straight for a long time, until he was certain that he was in, and then he'd work you over. If a spinner bowled with mid-off and mid-on up he'd smash them, get a man back and then rotate the strike, but otherwise he rarely hit the ball in the air. So if you were looking for caught covers, caught mid-offs, caught mid-ons, you were dreaming.

If you're raised in South Africa, you need to handle the short ball well, and he did. He wasn't especially looking to come forward or go back, he played everywhere, and because he had amazing eyes he picked up length as quickly as anybody; he had no real weakness. You just had to go at the stumps and hope for a mistake early doors.

And then there's the bowling. Most of the time he just ran in and sent down line and length to hit the top of off stump – a heavy ball, but with little variation, and in short spells. But he also had a quick length ball and a very good bouncer – he was what I'd call an effort bowler – which meant you had to always be on your guard because he had a delivery in him that could hit you on the head.

Which is why, in my opinion, Kallis, King Kallis, is the

greatest player ever to have played the game. His ability to get runs, as many runs as he got, to get the wickets that he did in all forms of the game and wherever he played, is just incredible. He's the only man to have scored more than ten thousand Test runs – 13,289 in total, with the sixteenth-highest average of all time – and also taken two hundred Test wickets – 292 in total. Added to that, he hardly ever dropped a catch at second slip – his total of 200 is the third-highest of all time – and he's still playing in 2015, just before his fortieth birthday.

He could achieve all of that because he has such a simple, positive attitude. When the South Africa players came back to the dressing room after Australia had taken them for 434 in fifty overs, it was Kallis who said, right, the bowlers have done their job, they're ten runs short, and sure enough, they were. He is simply amazing.

5. Kumar Sangakkara

Some batters from the subcontinent have great records at home, but find it hard to get runs away because the conditions ask such different questions of them. All the guys from there whom I've selected have performed abroad as well, and that's the sign of a top player.

A top player like Kumar Sangakkara, whose Test average of 57.40 is, at the time of writing, the tenth-highest ever, and achieved in far more matches than all those above him.

But obviously, like all these guys, he's about far more than just numbers; he's a beautiful, simple, elegant batter.

Because he has such an excellent all-round game, Sangakkara scored plenty of runs in Australia, and though he struggled in England initially, on his final tour he made runs in every innings. That was almost nice to see, because you want the players you think are greats to prove themselves as greats, and now he has. That's why I'd put him just that little bit ahead of the magnificent Mahela Jayawardene, a lovely man whose technique wasn't quite as reliable when he played outside Asia.

Sangakkara's work ethic is second to none: he hits ball after ball after ball until he's sure that he's ready to go, which keeps his technique very simple. He plays in straight lines and, as a left-hander, punches deliveries right back to where they came from. Anything overpitched he'll drive, and he leaves the ball incredibly well – as a lefty, you've got to, and you've got to know where your off stump is. He does.

Against short stuff, he gets into great positions because he picks length so, so well. He plays the pull shot well, he plays the hook shot well, and he gets out of the way well.

Again, he's a fantastic guy – a complete winner and real gentleman, on the field and off it. He's also a brilliant thinker about the game, clever at manipulating fields, knowing when to attack and when to defend, and just generally playing situations perfectly. He's ridiculously calm, and you never know when he's feeling under pressure – he never gives anything away.

The other thing about Sanga is how long he bats. Again, at the time of writing, he has eleven Test double centuries – two more than Lara, and only Sir Don Bradman has more, with twelve. It's no coincidence that Mahela is fifth in that list; if you can bat for a long time in Sri Lanka, you can bat for a long time anywhere.

6. Andrew Flintoff

Bowls at 90 mph, whacks it out of the ground, a gun slip fielder and a really good competitor. What more do you want?

I know that Jimmy Anderson has more wickets, and has been brilliant over a longer period, but Freddie's pace meant he was less reliant on conditions, and on the biggest stage he produced for us. His performance in that 2005 Ashes series was one of the best I've ever seen from a cricketer. On the Saturday evening at Edgbaston, he got the ball to reverse-swing both ways, bowling one of the best overs I've ever seen, and then on the Sunday morning at the Oval he bowled one of the best spells I've ever seen.

He also killed Adam Gilchrist, coming around the wicket and angling the ball away from him – pretty similar to the way people knocked over Strauss for the last part of his career. Gilly said he'd never faced anything better.

Basically, Freddie could do everything. He bowled fast, he bowled from either angle, he reverse-swung it, he was brilliant to left-handers, he bowled long spells, he didn't go for runs, and he not only got great players out, but worked them over. Not stuff you can measure in numbers, but who cares? When you speak to batters around the world, they all talk about when Freddie was on, and if you ask them about the hardest challenge they faced, about who really made them feel like they were in a battle, a lot of them will say him.

And that's the thing with Freddie. He didn't produce that kind of quality for as long as the very best players do, but when he was at his best he couldn't have been much better.

His batting, though not as consistent, was the same: on his day, he would destroy you. He probably didn't get the numbers that you'd want or expect, but his 50s, 60s and 70s were brutal and crucial. He's a guy who could win a game for you in a session with bat or ball, but even more than that, he just had the knack of doing the one thing that needed to be done, when it needed to be done – like running Ponting out with a direct hit in the final Test of the 2009 Ashes.

But his influence wasn't just on the pitch: he was also a talisman for the crowd. He was Freddie, he was the drinker, and everybody related to him, especially in England, which is a cool quality to have. So he could get the crowd going and into the game, get the Barmy Army singing and shouting, and that got him up, got us up, and had an effect on the opposition.

To see him now, with the body and the physique and the

fitness that he's got, he's in great shape, which makes me wonder if he got the best out of his ability. If he'd looked after himself better he might have been more consistent over the course of his career, but of all the bowlers I played with, he was still by far the hardest to face.

7. Adam Gilchrist (wk)

What I really love about Gilly is that he always played the same way: he wanted to come in and destroy you. He's a match-winner, an incredibly positive player, as well as a lovely, friendly guy.

You could see that he wasn't just a slogger, that he had serious technique, by the way he came in at the top of the order in one-day cricket and whacked the new ball. The only bowler I ever saw get on top of him was Freddie, but the way that Freddie bowled in that Ashes series was frightening for anyone.

His keeping was also pretty good. I know that batting is becoming more and more important, but you've still got to be a very good gloveman.

Your keeping and your batting both have to be A-grade, but a greater attribute still is having the ability to attack, the ability to take the game away from an opposition. Gilchrist invented that. His innings against Panesar at Perth in 2006 was just outstanding, and he had that ability, coming in after guys like Langer, Hayden, Ponting, Martyn and Clarke, to finish you in a session, to finish you dead, which he did on a number of occasions.

It's not surprising that he could pick up and pull well, seeing as he was brought up in Perth, on the bounciest wicket in the world, and he also hit fast bowlers down the ground with ease. But the thing that makes Gilchrist stand out, even among all the brilliant guys in this team, was how well he hit over the top. He was so positive that way; it was as if he thought, there are no fielders in the air so they can't catch me. Immense.

8. Shane Warne (c)

There's not much more I can say about Warnie. I've gone for him ahead of Murali, who's my twelfth man, because although he didn't bowl that well in India, he did a lot better there than Murali did in Australia: thirty-four wickets in seventeen innings at 43.11, with a best of 6–125, versus twelve wickets in nine innings at 75.41, with a best of 3–55.

Warne would be my captain. That's partly because everybody says he was the greatest captain Australia never had, but also because having been captained by him, and having spent so many hours talking cricket with him, I know that his ability to pick out weaknesses and then hammer them was special.

Michael Vaughan was magnificent in the way that he went about his business, but Warne had an incredible ability to take the opposition's negatives and turn them into your positives. He just knew how to get at particular people, and how to build pressure.

Also, Warne was a winner; he never, ever thought about defeat. He always talked about the positive option and he always took the positive option, because he knew that most of the time it would work. As soon as you go positively at somebody, that somebody's on the back foot. As soon as you go positively at a team, that team's on the back foot. Everything he does, he does at 100 mph, nothing in slow motion.

His approach was infectious. When somebody's that confident and that great, it encourages you to do the same. It brings out the best in you because you want to perform for the guy, you want to do well and you want him to talk positively about the way you play the game. His approval means something.

9. Jimmy Anderson

Jimmy is one of the most skilful bowlers I've ever seen. He has a brilliant wrist, which enables him not only to swing the ball both ways, but to control that swing; so if conditions offer any help, he is extremely hard to play.

But even when there's minimal movement through the air, he can use the pitch to cause trouble. His wobble-seam delivery allows him to hurry batters into shots, and on an abrasive track his command of reverse swing, along with his ability to hide the ball, means that he's dangerous all day.

Jimmy is also an excellent tactician. He's good at identifying faults in opponents and devising plans to knock them over, not just before games but out in the middle. We saw this in the 2015 Ashes at Edgbaston, when, very quickly, he realised that seam, rather than swing, was the way to take wickets. He ended up taking six of them, as Australia were skittled for 136 in 36.4 overs.

A superb athlete, Jimmy hardly ever misses a game, can bowl long spells, and is very good in the field.

10. Shoaib Akhtar

I might have gone for Mohammad Asif here, who could have been one of the best ever. But he gave up his best years, and even though he was brilliant, given what he did, I just can't select him.

Instead, I've gone for Shoaib. As with all of my bowlers, I've already explained most of what it is that made Shoaib so good. He was incredibly fast, swung the new ball and the old ball, and his overs and spells were an event. I'd use him in the same way Michael Clarke used Mitchell Johnson: in very short spells, to bowl super-aggressively. I'd set very attacking fields and ask him to bowl as quickly as possible and send down a few short balls. Enjoy!

11. Glenn McGrath

A great wicket-taker who dismissed the best batters. His ability to bore you out was phenomenal, and he hardly ever bowled a bad delivery – he knew he'd send down twenty overs in a day for forty or fifty runs, and that he'd get people out because of the pressure that created. Throw in the occasional jaffa, and he was even harder to handle.

What was also amazing was the way he led that Australian attack – everybody knew that McGrath was the man. He controlled and looked after all their bowlers, which is why we were all so happy when he went down at Edgbaston in 2005.

It was so hard to score off him, guys would have to play more aggressively against Lee and Gillespie – that's where they'd see their scoring opportunities. So even when he wasn't bowling, he was effective.

And McGrath also had an amazing partnership with Warne. The two of them were able to tie batsmen down so that the Test match didn't really go anywhere when they were on, and you couldn't afford that, because at some stage there was going to be good ball in there for you. You had to force the play, which brought mistakes, which brought wickets.

On the Future

We have an amazing sport, but to keep it amazing we need to take care of it. We need to take care of the people who play it, and the people who pay to watch it. If we do that, we'll be able to ensure our game remains attractive for the current generation of youngsters whose attention is being grabbed by other sports, video games, the internet or television.

Everyone in the sport, myself very much included, has a huge responsibility to make it the best it can possibly be.

I grew up with cricketers as my heroes and I speak to so many children now who say the same about the likes of Freddie Flintoff, Jimmy Anderson, Charlotte Edwards and the rest of the players in the England sides. These are the foundations we need to build upon to ensure the next generation become the sporting heroes to others later down the line.

What we have to do is prolong our great cricketers' careers. You don't want them to be away to broadcasting or coaching at thirty-four, thirty-five, and fast bowlers even earlier. You want the best guys to be able to play for a lot longer because they bring excitement, they bring entertainment and they bring fans, so we need to look after them.

You can be sure that it's on players' minds. They're worried about the longevity of their career, they want to get the most out of their talent, they want to be at their best all the time.

There needs to be enough cricket so that they say, yep, that's perfect. I can play in everything if I'm picked for everything, because it's not too taxing on my body. It's going to be hard because cricket is hard, but I'm not worrying that I can't cope with the schedule. Then we can see the very best of these guys every time they play.

We have a few genuine greats in the game at the moment – Steyn, Anderson, de Villiers and maybe Johnson. But we need to give guys like Root, Amla, Williamson and Kohli the best chance of getting themselves to that level as well.

And we also need to think of the public. Currently, there's too much cricket for them as well – we can't let it get boring, watching the same players day in, day out, seeing the same faces on TV all the time. In England, we should play one five-match Test series in the summer and one in the winter; we need to keep things special.

If there was less cricket, touring teams could arrive a little earlier and get used to conditions, then maybe we'd see more series going down to the wire. There are lots of reasons why Australia were thrashed in the 2015 Ashes, as there were when they thrashed us in 2013/14, but it's worth mentioning that, before they even got to England, they'd been away for three weeks on another series, playing three Tests against the West Indies, and by the time they get home, those who play limited overs will have been abroad for a third of the year straight. That is not normal, and it's not conducive to success either.

You hear people say, well, it's a fun job and they're well-paid – I'd like to have it. And they're completely right. Some of the best days of my life have been spent playing cricket and I'm incredibly lucky and privileged to have been paid to be there. But none of that changes how much you love and miss your family, none of that changes what the human body and mind are capable of, or the amount of rest they need to keep functioning at their peak.

Of course, you can talk over FaceTime and see each other that way, but a player wants to share all the stuff that happens with their family, so getting that balance right is really important, and it's one of the challenges within the game at the moment.

International cricket, and Test cricket in particular, is

hugely demanding – on fast bowlers especially. Backs, knees, ankles, sides, shoulders and all joints: you hear the guys who do it complain about pretty much every part of their body, and with good reason. I'm so glad I never had the attributes to be a fast bowler!

Even if you're a batter, spinner or wicketkeeper, it's tough to play for five days. It takes a serious amount of focus, endurance and fitness, which is extremely tiring, and so is the preparation you have to do to be ready for it.

I'm afraid that it looks like the only way to do this is to play less one-day cricket. Obviously the World Cup will stay, and the most recent one was fascinating, like a longer form of T20, and that's the way I'd go to fill the gaps – more T20.

As for Test cricket, we need to keep attendances up. You see the crowds around the world and, apart from in England and Australia, where the public are consistently incredible with supporting and attending sport, relatively few people go to watch it. When I went and did a Q&A at my son's school, the kids didn't even ask about it! Eleven- and twelve-year-olds only wanted to learn about the switch hit and hitting sixes. The coach is a good buddy of mine and he's finding it hard to get them to defend and to block – all they want to do is hit a six first ball. That's a sign of where the game is going. We want kids growing up understanding that Test cricket is the ultimate and that T20 can go hand in hand with it. I'm sure we can do it.

On the other hand, I'm sure most kids who play football

don't start off wanting to be goalkeepers and defenders, and of course they prefer attacking to defending – I do myself. But we need to make sure we teach and encourage them to discover how much enjoyment they can get from the longer form, and players who've benefited from Test cricket owe it to the game to talk it up whenever they can – especially if they've played a lot of T20 as well.

Groundsmen also have a huge responsibility and are often overlooked as a vital cog in protecting and enhancing our wonderful game. They have the ability to keep Test matches entertaining, by producing wickets conducive to entertaining cricket. The aggressive way that players are playing now means that you're not going to get that many boring draws, even on boring wickets – we saw that at Cardiff during the 2015 Ashes.

In England, we can make sure this happens if the groundsmen work for the ECB. That way, they can be told to prepare flat tracks for Tests, and for first-class cricket too.

This would help develop pace bowlers as they'd know all the tricks of getting good players out on good wickets. It would help the selectors too; more players of international standard would emerge undoubtedly.

I'd suggest reducing the number of counties and the amount of games our domestic guys play in a season. Quicks are expected to last from April to September, but they're knackered by the middle of the season and bowling at nowhere near full pace.

If we had fewer teams they could go flat out all the way

through, you could prepare for four-day games like they were Test matches, and you'd play a T20 tournament during the school summer holidays, promoting the game to the next generation who haven't otherwise been involved in cricket and showing kids there's life beyond the football season. Test cricket would ultimately benefit as participation would no doubt rise. The talent within our selection pool would increase the quality at every level in the country.

Instead of counties, we could take cities and regions instead, and pick teams from bigger pools. Let's say you made nine franchises; that gives every team eight fixtures, and the players who don't make it can strengthen second-team or minor-counties cricket. Then, if you get a guy coming back from injury, if he's trying to get back into the national team or struggling for form, there's a game for him against decent opposition.

I understand one of the problems with having a franchise system in England is rivalry between cities and football teams. People from both Manchester and Liverpool support Lancashire, but they're not about to support a franchise unless its name stays the same, each city has a team, or it's called something like North West. And you'd get the same in Yorkshire too, with Leeds and Sheffield.

In theory, the big issue would be upsetting the members who've been attached to their counties for years, and of course I understand the dilemma here, but I don't think there's any way around it. Ultimately, though, they are the bedrock of the game over here and I'm sure once they recognised it was for the best of the sport, they'd continue to support the game like they always have.

Whatever happens, the ECB, and all the other boards, have a responsibility to use their money well. It's not an easy job, I know, but they're making enough of it – certainly in England, India and Australia – to continue to make a difference. So as well as rewarding crowds for sticking with Test cricket, it could be used to reward the players as well. Make Test cricket the pinnacle of the sport in every sense and able to compete with the other global competitions.

In England this isn't so much of a problem, and they've realised the importance of the IPL – Eoin Morgan, England's limited-overs captain, was allowed to miss a one-day international to play for Sunrisers Hyderabad, which says it all. But what needs to happen now is for everyone to get together and block off time in the calendar when there will be no international cricket, so that everyone who's selected can play the full competition. And in return, the IPL needs to be a bit shorter – a month, not six weeks.

I'm not sure, though, whether this would sort out the issues they have in the West Indies, something I'm asked about a lot because I've played in the Caribbean for a couple of years. What I'd say is that the CPL is important, because it's getting people interested in the game again, and bringing crowds back. For quite a few years now, the West Indies haven't played the amazing cricket they have in the past, and they're not producing the kind of superstars they did in the seventies, eighties and early nineties. The CPL isn't going to change that immediately.

But the West Indies could have a really competitive Test team if the major stars started playing again. Chris Gayle, Dwayne Bravo, Kieron Pollard, Sunil Narine, Lendl Simmons and Darren Sammy all played in the IPL during their 2015 home series against England, and not just because they got paid well. This was a genuine matter of principle.

Ultimately they felt let down, and decided they didn't need the West Indies Cricket Board. I get that, but I also think there has to be some sort of an agreement where they can work together, because it's so important that the game has a strong West Indies team. Cricket is part of what makes the Caribbean such a wonderful, vibrant place and truly one of the best places in the world to both play and watch the game.

I spoke to Jason Holder about this recently, and told him that it's the job of the captain to get the senior players in a room and ask them to come back. Then he has to ask them help him run the team, which will benefit him as a leader.

But he also needs to ask them how they are all going to make West Indies cricket better. To ask, how are we going to make youngsters want to be us? How are we going to create one standard in the dressing room where everybody strives for one thing, where everyone's a leader?

Once those guys show that they're willing to talk, it's up to the administrators. What they need to realise is that spectators go to watch players, not them. They're there to serve the game, and not the other way around.

Yes, you need a governing body, but in this case it would help if they took a backward step and actually asked for advice from experienced professionals who are either still playing or have recently finished to understand what's going on. Look at the MCC's World Cricket Committee: Rod Marsh, Pollock, Ponting, Sangakkara, Vaughan, Adams, Sourav Ganguly, Ramiz Raja, Tim May, Mike Brearley and Charlotte Edwards, people who know what's what. This group has experienced pretty much all there is to experience in the sport and their knowledge and expertise should be utilised as much as possible.

One thing I disagree with those guys about, though, is that we need to have night-time Test matches. Test cricket should not be touched.

In the first place, I don't think it's going to make any difference at all to attendances. People might want to be there to begin with because it's a historic occasion, or a novelty, but I'm talking about after that. Who's going to watch a Test match on a week night? At eight or nine o'clock I want to be at home, not spending five days at the Adelaide Oval, whether I'm playing or watching.

There are other problems too. We've been playing Tests since 1877, in the same conditions. Are you going to say, we're going to start a whole new set of statistics, because people think that day–night cricket's great?

In most places, as soon as the sun goes down the temperature drops, and then when the lights are involved the wicket speeds up – you get a kind of glare on the surface, and the ball skids on. It's weird to have that change on every day of a Test, and it's not right that halfway through days four and five the ball would stop spinning when it should be spinning more, all the more so because it's wet with dew and harder to grip.

On the other hand, something that would really improve Test cricket is a Test World Championship. When they first started talking about that I was really excited, because it was going to be at the forefront of everybody's thinking and would give everyone an aim. It would also make more money for the players – another reason for them to prioritise the format.

What I'd do is split the ten nations into two groups, and over two years they'd play each other home and away, with points awarded for wins and draws. Then the top team in each group would get home advantage for a semi-final Test against the second-placed team in the other group, and the winners would meet in the final at a predetermined ground that changes every time. It might be tricky to work out, but I'm certain that it's not impossible, and that it'd be great.

Instead, we're seeing too many series involving England, Australia and India. South Africa, Sri Lanka and New Zealand have wonderful cricketers who deserve to be playing against the best players from the other nations – I don't think that, just because of television rights and the financial structure, some teams should get better opportunities than others. It's not right and it's not sport. The rich need to look after the poor.

The same applies to the crazy decision to limit the World

Cup to ten nations. Ireland and the Netherlands have beaten traditional powers; Zimbabwe, Bangladesh and Sri Lanka haven't always played Tests. The more the so-called lesser countries compete at international level, the more they'll improve and the more the game grows. All of them have players of international standard, and it's ludicrous to ban them from exploiting their talent just because of where they were born. I like equality, I like fairness; that isn't equal or fair. And besides, as the Rugby World Cup has demonstrated, unexpected and extraordinary things can happen in David and Goliath encounters.

So there are lots of ways we can improve things, and we should always be looking for them. We're competing for people's time and money with so many other sports and hobbies. But actually, none of the things we need to do are particularly difficult to do. As long as we have people running the game who care about it, and speak to people who know about it, we have an amazing future to enjoy and look forward to.

And one thing we should never, ever forget is how wonderful the game already is, and to appreciate and enjoy it as much as we can.

Acknowledgements

I'm hugely grateful once again to the great many people who help bring a project like this to life. At Mission Sports Management, Adam Wheatley and Nick Hartwell have been brilliantly supportive, as always. Daniel Harris is a truly talented writer and has worked tirelessly with me to set my thoughts on the game down on paper. And I'd like to thank my publisher Adam Strange and his exceptional team at Sphere; particularly Zoe Gullen, Marie Hrynczak, Stephanie Melrose and Maddie Mogford.

Picture Credits

Nick Potts/PA Archive/PA Images: 1 (*top*)

Rebecca Naden/PA Archive/PA Images: 1 (*bottom*)

David Munden/Popperfoto/Getty Images: 2 (*top*)

Adrian Murrell/Allsport/Getty Images: 2 (*bottom*)

PA/PA Wire/PA Images: 3 (*top*)

Adam Davy/PA Archive/PA Images: 3 (*bottom*)

REX Shutterstock: 4 (*top*)

Hamish Blair/Getty Images: 4 (*bottom*), 5 (*top*), 23 (*top right*)

Gurinder Osan/AP/PA Images: 5 (*bottom*)

Ian Kington/Getty Images: 6 (*top*)

Tom Shaw/Getty Images: 6 (*bottom*), 9, 20 (*top*), 22 (*bottom left*), 23 (*middle left*)

Mark Kolbe/Getty Images: 7 (*top*)

David Rowe/Demotix/PA Images: 7 (*bottom*)

Alessandro Abbonizio/Getty Images: 8

Julian Herbert/Getty Images: 10 (*top*)

Bob Thomas/Popperfoto/Getty Images: 10 (*bottom*)

Christopher Lee/Getty Images: 11 (*top*)

Alexander Joe/Getty Images: 11 (*bottom*)

Ashley Allen/Getty Images: 12 (*top*)

AFP Photo/STRINGER/Getty Images: 12 (*bottom*)

Robert Cianflone/Getty Images: 13 (*top*)

Daniel Munoz/Getty Images: 13 (*bottom*)

Gareth Copley/PA Archive/PA Images: 14 (*top*)

Laurence Griffiths/Getty Images: 14 (*bottom*)

Ryan Pierse/Getty Images: 15 (*inset*), 18 (*bottom*)

Quinn Rooney/Getty Images: 15 (*main picture*)

Rob Griffith/AP/PA Images: 16

Patrick Eagar/Getty Images: 17, 19 (*top*)

Robert Prezioso/Getty Images: 18 (*top*)

Hamish Blair–IPL 2010/Getty Images: 19 (*bottom*)

Morne de Klerk/Getty Images: 20 (*bottom*)

Prakash Singh/Getty Images: 21 (*top*)

Gareth Copley/Getty Images: 21 (*bottom*)

Lucas Dawson/Getty Images: 22 (*top left*)

British Sky Broadcasting Ltd/REX Shutterstock: 22 (*top right*)

Mark Nolan/Getty Images: 22 (*middle left*)

Gallo Images/Getty Images: 22 (*middle right*)

Clive Brunskill/Getty Images: 22 (*bottom right*)

Jonathan Wood/Getty Images: 23 (*top left*)

Pradeep Mandhani/Getty Images: 23 (*middle right*)

John Gichigi/Getty Images: 23 (*bottom left*)

Mike Hewitt/Allsport/Getty Images: 23 (*bottom right*)

Paul Kane/Getty Images: 24